11/10

MYTH, RITUAL A

C000050301

Jack Goody is one of the pre-eminent social scientists in the world. Over the past half-century his pioneering writings at the intersections of anthropology, history and social and cultural studies have made him one of the most widely read, most widely cited and most widely translated scholars working today.

In *Myth, Ritual and the Oral,* he returns to the related themes of myth, orality and literacy, subjects that have long been a touchstone in anthropological thinking. Combining classic papers with recent unpublished work, this volume brings together some of the most important essays written on these themes in the past half-century, representative of a lifetime of critical engagement and research. In characteristically clear and accessible style, Jack Goody addresses fundamental conceptual schemes underpinning modern anthropology, providing potent critiques of current theoretical trends. Drawing upon his highly influential work on the LoDagaa myth of the Bagre, Goody challenges structuralist and functionalist interpretations of oral 'literature', stressing the issues of variation, imagination and creativity, and the problems of methodology and analysis. These insightful, and at times provocative, essays will stimulate fresh debate and prove invaluable to students and teachers of social anthropology.

JACK GOODY is Emeritus Professor of Social Anthropology in the University of Cambridge and a Fellow of St John's College. Knighted by Her Majesty The Queen for services to anthropology, Professor Goody has researched and taught all over the world, is a fellow of the British Academy, and in 1980 was made a Foreign Honorary member of the American Academy of Arts and Sciences. In 2004 he was elected to the National Academy of Sciences and he was elected Commandeur des Arts et Lettres in 2006.

MYTH, RITUAL AND THE ORAL

JACK GOODY

CAMBRIDGE
UNIVERSITY PRESS

CAMBRIDGE UNIVERSITY PRESS
Cambridge, New York, Melbourne, Madrid, Cape Town, Singapore,
São Paulo, Delhi, Dubai, Tokyo, Mexico City

Cambridge University Press
The Edinburgh Building, Cambridge CB2 8RU, UK

Published in the United States of America by Cambridge University Press, New York

www.cambridge.org
Information on this title: www.cambridge.org/9780521128032

First published 2010

Printed in the United Kingdom at the University Press, Cambridge

A catalogue record for this publication is available from the British Library

Library of Congress Cataloguing in Publication data
Goody, Jack.
Myth, ritual and the oral / Jack Goody.
p. cm.
Includes bibliographical references and index.
ISBN 978-0-521-76301-1 (hardback) – ISBN 978-0-521-12803-2 (pbk.)
1. Oral tradition. 2. Folklore–Performance. 3. Storytelling. 4. Ritual. I. Title.
GR72.3.G66 2010
398.2–dc22
2010033389

ISBN 978-0-521-76301-1 Hardback
ISBN 978-0-521-12803-2 Paperback

Contents

Acknowledgements   *page* vi

Introduction   1

1 Religion and ritual from Tylor to Parsons:
   the definitional problem   13

2 Oral 'literature'   41

3 The anthropologist and the audio recorder   58

4 Oral creativity   64

5 The folktale and cultural history   70

6 Animals, humans and gods in northern Ghana   84

7 The Bagre in all its variety   95

8 From oral to written: an anthropological breakthrough
   in storytelling   117

9 Writing and oral memory: the importance
   of the 'lecto-oral'   153

Appendix. Folktales in northern Ghana   162

References   167

Index   174

Acknowledgements

I am grateful to Juliet Mitchell for her help and encouragement, to Mark Offord, Mel Hale and Sue Mansfield for their assistance with the manuscript, as well as to Gilbert Lewis and to Stephen Hugh-Jones for our seminar and the latter's comments, and to the memory of Kum Gandah, Ian Pierre Watt and Meyer Fortes, to all of whom (and others) I am indebted, including the typists and data processors who have helped with the various versions of the Bagre, as well as to the readers and editor of Cambridge University Press.

The essays, for which I thank the publishers for allowing a reprinting in slightly altered form, have appeared as follows:

Religion and ritual: the definitive problem. *British Journal of Sociology* 12 (1961).

Oral literature. *Encyclopaedia Britannica* (forthcoming).

The coming of the tape recorder. *Médium* (2005).

Oral creativity (forthcoming).

The folktale and cultural history. Oralité et Littérature: échos, écarts, resurgences. *Cahiers de Littérature Orale* 56 (2005).

Animals, men and gods in northern Ghana. *Cambridge Anthropology* 16 (1992/3).

The Bagre in all its variety. Introduction to *A Myth Revisited: The Third Bagre* (with S. W. D. K. Gandah) (Carolina Academic Press, 2003).

From oral to written: an anthropological breakthrough in story-telling. In *Il Romanzo*, vol. 1, *La cultura del romanzo*, ed. F. Moretti (Turin: Einaudi, 2001. In English, Princeton University Press).

Writing and oral memory. Lecture, Berne, Switzerland, June 2007.

Introduction

In this short volume I am not trying to say anything I have not said before. I am going back to a number of articles because, especially with my repeated recording of the Bagre, there is a problem which has brought me up against many discussions of 'myth', oral 'literature' and their relation to other aspects of social life. The whole discussion had become incrusted with a mystical quality which my own observations did little to confirm. Since I spent such a large part of my career in recording, transcribing and translating the various versions of LoDagaa 'myth' or recitation (together with my friend from the area, Kum Gandah), it seemed worthwhile trying to bring together some of these general observations.

The subject of myth and ritual has been of fundamental interest to anthropologists (and others) from the very beginning. They were supposed to have formed part of the characteristics of 'primitive society', like animism (the worship of nature) and euhemerism (the worship of the dead). As such they are features of 'other cultures', outside the bounds of 'modern' rationality, obeying another system of logic, or indeed being 'pre-logical', 'irrational' in our terms. I have wanted to adopt a more cognitive approach, partly because of my interest in communication, especially in orality and literacy, than is possible in the usual 'functional' and 'structural' (or post-structural) approaches to such activities. But there are others too. In this I recognize the logic, as Evans-Pritchard did for the Azande, of looking at the societies more from the actor's point of view, and considering such forms not as a fixed, formulaic product but as reflecting man's creativity, as a language-using animal in face of the world, not free from tradition but not bound down by it.

I do not wish to claim to be the only one to adopt a different approach. There are indeed a number of writers who have focussed on poetics and linguistics and have taken stock of variants, though I do not think that this approach has yet had much of an impact, not on the nature of 'primitive mentalities'. Others have stressed the social context of narrative and the dialogical relations between narrator and audience, the evidence for which was relatively thin in earlier days before the audio recorder. It is this that can bring out variants which occur not only within a 'structure' but which vary in some unpredictable ways. In this sense they are creative.

The analysis of myth and ritual had been one of the major themes of anthropology, going back to Frazer and *The Golden Bough*,[1] to Malinowski in his writings on the Trobriands,[2] to Radcliffe-Brown in the study of the Andamans,[3] and above all to Claude Lévi-Strauss in his work on totemism and in *The Savage Mind* and *Mythologiques*.[4] For these and many writers (less so with Malinowski), the analysis of these behavioural forms has been a major touchstone of anthropological thought, but they have also characterized the 'primitive mind' – for example, in the work of the philosopher Ernst Cassirer, on mytheopoeic thinking. I argue along the lines of Malinowski, who attempted to show that in fishing expeditions the Trobriands distinguished between the technical and the ritual, between those operations that required the participation of transcendental powers and those that did not (although presumably all could benefit from whatever source). 'Rational' and non-rational action were both present among the 'primitives' as with us.

Nevertheless, the subjects of this study are by no means unambiguous, whether myth or ritual (or even 'orality'). Many have different views about what they are. Some have seen 'myth' as consisting of a specific recital, as in the case of the Bagre of the LoDagaa. In this usage the term refers to a particular recitation of a long account of the beginning of things (myth 1). As our work shows, there can be surprising variants over time and speaker, even down to features of the basic outlook, which is highly significant for the study of mythologies – never so fixed as a single version suggests. Here the importance of the

[1] Frazer 1890.   [2] Malinowski 1922.   [3] Radcliffe-Brown 1952.
[4] Lévi-Strauss 1964, 1966, 1969.

portable audio recorder comes into the picture because it enables you to register (and to write down and compare) innumerable recitations and to analyse the variants. This problem is complicated. Yes, all variations are made within a 'common frame'. But what is this? When I first recorded the Bagre I was convinced (because the LoDagaa told me) that the recitations were 'one' (*boyen*), the same. So they were for LoDagaa. All were recited in the same ritual situation. But even the initial invocation, learnt 'by heart', varied, and the recitations themselves differed not only in detail but in entire outlook, in worldview. Are these still within 'a common frame'? I would argue, no. Others may disagree. But changes in a recitation can be very radical, in a generative way, leading to something 'other'. You do not go back to the discipline of a written text but proceed in a chain-like way; the last version is always the starting point. To see this process as nothing more than transformations within a frame seems to me to underestimate their extent, or else to comprehend it all within a 'boy meets girl' formula, as I believe Propp does with folktales,[5] thus failing to recognize the creativity of oral cultures. Variations in oral recitations may be recognized by anthropologists, though dominant models would want to restrict these to 'variations within a frame', whereas my argument is that one can never know where these variations might lead until one records and examines them, even if they are in the hands of a ritual specialist, a shaman or even a remembrancer. In any case, one always has to ask what is the purpose of remembering exactly, of denying creativity, which is an ability that comes 'naturally' with the use of words, to language-using minds?

Others see myth too as a 'mythology' (myth 2), which includes ideas about man and the supernatural emanating from a plurality of sources and is essentially put together by an individual, usually an outsider. For a structuralist like Lévi-Strauss, it is the whole body of mythology that constitutes a unity for analysis, one which is constructed from multiple sources; I refer to this as mythology, the mythology of the Nambikwara or of the LoDagaa which, as I have indicated, may be more complex and variable than the idea of the 'ethnographic present' suggests, for this notion depends upon the acceptance of an unchanging past.

[5] Propp 1968.

Lévi-Strauss himself goes further and calls into question the status of the myth (2) of discrete societies, though this refers not primarily to a recitation but to a transcendental view of the world. The mythology of the Nambikwara forms part of the mythology of their neighbours and vice versa in an endless series of transformations that have, for him, 'no initial starting point'. A 'transformation' implies a common 'form', but that must be in the eye of the observer, not with the 'actor' frame of reference. So the 'mythology of the Nambikwara' would be an 'illusionary entity'. However, it did constitute an entity of sorts as it was collected from a specific group. And, as I have remarked, it is something very different from myth (1),[6] an actual recitation like the *Iliad*. Lévi-Strauss has shifted somewhat over time from the analysis of a particular myth in its social or transcendental context to cross-continental transformation.[7] Variations obviously occur, but they are always within a framework, the existence of which I dispute as such 'structures' are an illusory entity.

It has been pointed out to me that 'myth' may vary on a continental scale, African in contrast to South American, with which Lévi-Strauss is dealing. That is certainly a possibility, but I would stress the difference here between myth and mythology as well as remarking that folktales and 'myths' have crossed from continent to continent, the Ananse tales in the first instance and the Muslim and Christian story in the second. There are points of contact between the two and there are some quasi-universal (European-derived) concepts and explanations which he himself has tried to refine, e.g. with regard to totems. There are of course dangers in commenting on the concept of totemism from an Africanist standpoint, but there are also some conceptual advantages and in any case the task is necessary if one regards anthropology as a general field, as our forefathers did – at the same time recognizing the role of 'local knowledge'.

Other people refer to a specific story, in one of its versions or in all, as a myth (myth 3). An example of this usage is the story of Oedipus, to which there is clearly more than one approach. The first analyses a written version about a specific character, as it appears in, say, a Greek text (or possibly from a plurality, as Robert Graves does). A second

[6] Stephen Hugh-Jones personal correspondence.
[7] I am indebted for this observation to Stephen Hugh-Jones.

is to do as Jacobs does, look at the way a particular story has developed over the ages, which is the basis for her study *On Matricide*.[8] Then there is the more cultural (in a different sense) approach of Dumézil to Indo-European myth,[9] an area into which Lévi-Strauss also moves in his *Mythologiques*, considering all versions from one 'culture area' as being in some sense variants one of another. But this enquiry is also based on the 'structural approach' to myth (myth 2) as understood by Lévi-Strauss. What Jacobs takes from him is the understanding that myths reveal the 'underlying "universal" unconscious structures', that is, those of 'underlying "rules" or "laws"';[10] a study of a body of myths will show universal structures. However, the understanding of matricide as a quasi-universal feature is questionable, both for myth and for 'reality'. Taken literally, the practice seems a quite distinct development, related to intergenerational tensions within the family. As such, it will appear in both patrilineal and matrilineal societies; indeed, in some relevant respects these resemble each other. The inheritance of 'male' goods and the succession to 'male' office may pass through women, but goes to men in both cases; indeed, most studies of matrilineal societies, for example by the anthropologists of the 1930s who were students of Malinowski (that is, Richards and Fortes), showed they were characterized by male authority. However, as the Bagre myth brings out so well at a more explicit level, in most societies (including, of course, bilateral ones) authority and responsibility at a domestic level are normally divided between male and female; both parents experience the wrath of their children, and in one version the child shoots the mother with an arrow. The binary approach of Lévi-Strauss, which would see these relationships as alternatives, is inappropriate; the 'family' ties of children with both father and mother exist in all types of society, though these may vary in intensity.

Jacobs, however, prefers a structuralist approach that emphasizes the 'hierarchical dualism' and the 'unconscious' element in myth and that leads her to draw attention to the non-appearance but importance of Metis in the Oresteian story. Although Athena says quite early in *Eumenides*, 'no mother gave me birth', Jacobs posits Metis as Athena's mother, a woman who has been raped (and swallowed)

---

[8] Jacobs 2007.   [9] Dumézil 1990 [1940].   [10] Jacobs 2007: 17.

by Zeus. If the introduction of the unconscious can allow one this degree of ingenuity in the analysis of myth, where does it stop?

The second type of study involves the analysis of a complete 'mythology', as Lévi-Strauss has advocated. There is an obvious problem here if we accept the results of our study of the Bagre since versions vary so much in a fundamental fashion. How is one to choose? Structural analysis along the lines of Lévi-Strauss is difficult because one can never know the entire universe of discourse, the dimensions of future and past myth. On the other hand, one can more easily carry out a study of past (written down, textualized) myths because writing produces a boundary to what we are examining; there is no such boundary to the Bagre as an oral performance because it is constantly being recited differently, so that, when it is written, one is always looking at an arbitrary sample. But if this is so of the Bagre, it must also have been true of the Greek case; what we have is only an arbitrary selection that has at one time been written down, leaving a plethora of potential versions 'in the air', which have been presented but not recorded. Listening to a recording can also produce a variety of written outcomes, as we can see from the Braimah recordings and as I know only too well from poring over the Bagre recordings for days on end with my friend Kum (the originals are deposited in St John's College library, Cambridge). It is essential to take into account the context in which written versions of 'oral' myth have been produced.

With reference to myth 3, one can select Oedipus rather than Prometheus as the key myth, as Jacobs does, but the selection is one's own, depending on one's particular social environment three thousand years later when Antiquity has given way to feudalism and then to 'capitalism'. One is no longer analysing a purely Greek myth but one that has been stripped down, shorn of its time-specific components and presented in its reduced state to be quasi-universal. So she undertakes an examination of Greek myths (supposedly oral) as treated in a written tradition and she comments on 'the cultural reception of myth in the present' rather than what the original may have meant to its audience. Myth is being used to theorize a supposedly underlying cultural law that is related to the symbolic in a post-Lacanian sense, the aim being to classify 'underlying "universal" unconscious structures'. Symbolic here is 'the order of meaning to which all human beings are subjected if they are to become part of the social world'.[11] The symbolic is structured 'through a hierarchical dualism'. But what are these underlying structures? In her case Jacobs wants to do more than analyse; she wants to change the order of things, so that the recognition of matricide is an attempt to rediscover a new (feminist) order. In other words, myth itself records the desiderata, what one wants, not simply what is.

I believe this form of cryptologic analysis to be mistaken. I cannot agree that myths are a mystery to the reciter who understands them only unconsciously, that they represent 'a code' and disregard 'the thinking subject completely',[12] but they reveal 'universal mental formulations'.[13] This position leads this particular writer to talk of myth as 'a form of delirium',[14] 'cultural delirium', and as equivalent to the dream, to a 'cultural dream'. But myth is not peculiar in this way simply because it is oral. It does not shed a particular light on the unconscious, like individual dreams; it must rather be compared to other forms of 'literature', to the conscious act of creation and imaginative productions – albeit of a 'traditional' kind. Believers in myth are not more 'delirious' than those who think that man's loss of heavenly grace was due to biting an apple, or that the world was created 'magically' in seven days.

Thirdly, we return to the study of a particular recitation (myth 1), where once again we have to face the question of a plurality of versions. We can call this the study of 'contemporary myth' since it is what is being recited now in relation to a current situation, not a resurrection of an earlier tale, as with Oedipus, nor of a nebulous totality. The 'contemporary myth' must clearly be interpreted in relation to the society from which it comes. One cannot envisage any other solution for an analysis of the Bagre. However, looking back to a written 'myth' presents different problems, especially where the elements are said to persist over time, as with Oedipus (that is, a particular story rather than a particular recitation). There may be some such persisting element in the Bagre, such as the conflict between parent and child, that encapsulates wider aspects of intergenerational relations and that represents some more permanent facets of

[11] Jacobs 2007: 18.   [12] Jacobs 2007: 16.   [13] Jacobs 2007: 17.
[14] Jacobs 2007: 19.

the human situation. This may well be the case with the story of Oedipus; it certainly was so for Freud, but it may not be universal in that form, as Malinowksi claimed to show. For the Oedipal situation is intergenerational, and yet hierarchical and sibling relationships differ significantly in matrilineal societies, for example. In any case one is not applying a 'structural' approach to myth because one is taking only one version of one element in the Greek mythology rather than reading that element in a wider context,[15] as Lévi-Strauss proposed. That is what we do when we select a tale from a written corpus and decide this to be a foundational element. It may embody a continuing aspect of some part of human life, as with the Oedipus story, but that we cannot know until time has passed and we see what endures. However, in the case of Oedipus we might equally regard the story not as myth but as an aspect of history (partially oral, in fact) and comparable, in a general way, to Prince Harry taking the crown from the brow of his dying father. That story too has few supernatural elements and encapsulates a general situation.

There is another input to this discussion that I have dealt with elsewhere at some length but now do so in a more limited way, and that is the effects of the advent of literacy on communication of this kind. This forms the subject of Chapters 8 and 9, where I have been concerned with the problem of narration, which some have seen as marking earlier (oral) cultures and some as an aspect of human discourse more generally. I have been less impressed in oral societies with the aspect of narrative, both imaginative and personal, at least in the sense of a sequential account of one's own and another's life experience, activities which seem to me promoted by the written word. In oral cultures, the occasions for the latter are limited and I have experienced imaginative storytelling largely for children, certainly as a distraction, not primarily relevant to 'real life' (although it may of course have some underlying 'truth'). Myth is very different, for that usually has a strongly religious and even explanatory role; it is not recited 'raw' round a campfire but to adults in a special ritual context.

One possibility with folktales, as my interlocutor reminds me, is the varying kind of interpretation as between children and adults.

[15] Jacobs 2007: 16.

Certainly, a literal (child's) understanding of the story about one's loss of immortality to the moon is different from an adult's, but I believe we can confidently conclude that in Europe, Africa and so many other parts the primary audience is infantile. Hugh-Jones sees a problem in the folktale–myth distinction for South America because the same story appears in different contexts and that is a feature we have to bear in mind elsewhere.[16]

If you are not looking at a particular 'myth', or even at a specific collection, you can be in all sorts of difficulty. Many stories about the gods, or of a supernatural character, vary among themselves (through the process of invention, forgetting and the production of variants that I have demonstrated to exist among the LoDagaa). To aggregate these different versions together may be very difficult; in the various versions of the Bagre, stories referring to the beginning of things may reflect not a single vision of the world but conflicting ones, depending on the individual in charge. Each version has to be looked at separately, even within one culture, the so-called worldview being more differentiated than most anthropologists with their vision of a single-stranded 'ethnographic present' can contemplate.

In these chapters I have tried to pull together my observations in a number of earlier essays, modified as occasion demands, on the subject of the myth and ritual, and on oral 'literary' activity and how that was affected by the written mode. I begin with an early essay defining traditional concepts of religion and ritual, which is not directly connected with 'literature' but attempts to look at the problem of setting aside a special category of ritual activity. It examines some classical statements of the question and offers some kind of reconciliation. The subsequent chapters are centred upon types of oral 'literature' (or rather standardized oral forms) and their transition to the written, because it is in this process that I see the original question of 'myth' as lying, the place it occupied in ancient Greece.

In a much earlier paper, Watt and I wrote of the Greek version of the myths in an early literate society as stories of the men of old (*mythos*) as distinct from the more modern *istoria*, characteristic of a written culture in which you could look back in a different way.[17] Myths then referred to tales in which one could no longer believe,

---

[16] Hugh-Jones personal correspondence.   [17] Goody 2009.

that were no longer accepted as in tune with a contemporary out-look, especially as regards the immorality of the gods. In going back to these stories, one is talking of tales of olden times, which have no particular status as regards today except, as I have remarked, that some of them deal with aspects of social life that persist over a variety of cultural contexts. But to think about this in terms of a continuing unconscious, as the collective unconscious, is mistaken; they cannot be treated like the products of an individual unconscious for there is no window and no glimpse of the unconscious through error in the way Freud has remarkably shown in *The Psychopathology of Everyday Life*, there can be no collective psychopathology, no mass slips of the tongue, not really much general vision through individual dreams (though some). In any case, how does one see that collective uncon-scious being transmitted down the ages? Only in the way that Lévi-Strauss sees other aspects of 'l'esprit human' as being reproduced, by a species of cultural parthenogenesis. At this level nothing (or everything) works.

However, following on the extensive work on the Bagre of the LoDagaa of northern Ghana, which I carried out in cooperation with my colleague over a period of many years, I was impressed not by the continuity over time of long recitations covering the transcen-dental world, but rather by their ability to change, not so much in accordance with the social structure generally (however defined) but with a more free-floating use of the creative imagination. This is to modify both the 'functional' and the 'structural' analysis of myth (at least in one main version, as with *Asdiwal*). Of course, the variation takes place within a context, but it is one much wider than would be suggested by these approaches and looks towards the composition of written literature rather than the hide-bound recitation of the same entity believed to exist by those who have recorded only one version; this is then seen in the context of a static 'primitive mentality'. On the contrary, they show signs of considering the problems connected with the supernatural in a manner not so very different from ours, the contribution of God as compared with that of 'the beings of the world', of what can be seen as 'evolution' as against 'creationism', in a simpler, less reflexive fashion than developed in later written, philo-sophical discourse but more or less present embryonically. These are competing accounts, held contemporarily rather than sequentially, the result of the flexible creativity of some, not all, oral cultures, as distinct from the relative fixity of written transcendentalism, where the 'word of God' is singular and repetitive. And it is only seen when the audio recorder and computer present us with the possibility of examining multiple recitations. The interaction between technology and analysis is a key aspect of my study of variation in parts of oral cultures just as writing was in literate ones.

Myth in this first sense is localized, the product of a particular intellectual environment. That is not at all the same with other oral forms with which it is often grouped, for example the folktale. I have argued that such tales involve a very different audience, both in oral societies and in literate ones where they continue to be recited – but largely to juvenile audiences, for entertainment, not to be taken at the same level of seriousness. Consequently, I see efforts to use these tales to determine adult 'mentalities', even as *disjecta membra* of myths, as being mistaken, both in oral and in written cultures. There is a further reason. The stories are short, easily memorized, and transmitted from society to society without a great deal of alteration. They are, in other words, international compared to the localized myth. They are therefore less responsive to variation in social structure, which is why folklorists have been able to identify them over large areas, and why I have been able to demonstrate them as minimally responsive to differences as between the LoDagaa and the Gonja social structures (see the Appendix). This internationalization has to do with the transmission of such tales across frontiers by the members of these societies themselves as well as not so much by wandering minstrels but by those few specialists who move from one village to another, even if only to sustain themselves on beer and porridge but also hoping for some gain, as in the case of the professional drummer at the courts of chiefs where their audience is frequently more localized, though we do have examples of those who move from one camp to another.

I have distinguished myth, legend and folktale on various grounds, but especially in the context of recital. Gilbert Lewis points out that in New Guinea, old ladies may recite all three varieties to children (and others),[18] but I would think of all three as folktales within these circumstances; the terms may merge in different contexts.

---

[18] Lewis 2000.

This then is what I offer as a contribution to the study of oral 'literature', to the study of myth, stressing the imaginative factor, individual 'creation', variability, and therefore the fundamental difficulty of analysis, along Malinowskian or Lévi-Straussian lines, psychological or sociological, that depends upon the notion of a single, fixed form, or even one that varies between certain limited parameters. A relatively fixed form and context does exist with folk-tales (and other short oral products) that can be easily memorized and transmitted not simply internally but externally too. But they have a very different, largely juvenile audience and the intention is to entertain although they also inform. As such, these are transmitted by storytellers rather than by ritual specialists.

CHAPTER I

Religion and ritual from Tylor to Parsons: the definitional problem

This first chapter represents an early attempt to sort out the problem surrounding the use of the terms ritual and religion. I tried to do the same for myth in a joint article (with Ian Watt). They are very much a preliminary to my specific analyses of the ethnographic material. I thought that later usage had not solved earlier problems and that we relied on a 'rationalist' view, despite attempts to avoid this.

To begin with I want to explore the problem of what has been involved in categorizing acts and beliefs as religious, or ritual, or magico-religious, with the purpose not only of clearing the way for subsequent treatment of my own empirical data (mainly concerning the LoDagaa and Gonja of northern Ghana), but also of clarifying certain aspects of the analysis of social systems in general.

For some writers such an investigation has appeared a profitless enterprise. At the beginning of *Themis: A Study of the Social Origins of Greek Religion*, a book which, as its subtitle suggests, owes much to the work of the French sociologist Durkheim, as well as to the English anthropologists, the classical scholar Jane Harrison comments on the erroneous approach of those inquirers who start with a general term *religion*, of which they have a preconceived idea, and then try to fit into it any facts that come to hand. Instead she proposes no initial definition, but remarks that 'we shall collect the facts that admittedly are religious and see from what human activities they appear to have sprung'.[1] It is yet more tempting for the inquirer into societies farther removed from our own tradition than that of ancient Greece to adopt a similar approach, and quietly to overlook the definitional problems. The dangers, however, outweigh the advantages.

---

[1] Harrison 1912: 29.

In refusing to define her field of discourse, Harrison was far from escaping the problem she perceived; she was merely taking refuge in an implicit rather than an explicit judgement of what constitutes the 'admittedly religious'. It goes without saying that such hidden decisions may influence the investigation of particular events. It might be possible to examine the funerals and Bagre performances of the LoDagaa without raising the wider issues were it not that the analysis of the specific data must depend, to some extent at least, upon the general position which the investigator takes with regard to them. Moreover, the difficulties which arise from a failure adequately to delimit one's universe of discourse become much more complicated when comparative studies are involved. With these matters in mind, therefore, I shall try and review some of the general discussions connected with the examination of what have variously and somewhat indiscriminately been described as ritual, ceremonial or religious phenomena.

In attempting to clarify these concepts for sociological purposes we are not trying to arrive at the fundamental meaning conveyed by the English term 'religion'. Not that we are indifferent to what Bohannan has called the folk-categories of European societies.[2] They form the inevitable starting point from which to develop one's analytic concepts. But normally they cannot themselves serve as such. In all branches of comparative social science this process of defining adequate categories has given birth to polemical problems of considerable magnitude, as witness the discussion which has arisen about the nature of the family or of legal, political and economic institutions. And the progress of studies of kinship systems, to take one such example, has to a significant degree depended upon distinguishing among the various connotations of the contemporary English concept of the 'family' in the light of investigations in other societies, and then giving more restricted technical meanings for this and other words when they are used for comparative analysis. The results of such endeavours may make ethnological reports more tedious to the general reader. While this is to be regretted, it can be avoided only at the expense of the development of the study of human institutions.

---

[2] Bohannan 1957.

In this analysis of the various approaches to the definition of religious and ritual phenomena, I shall begin with the nineteenth-century contributions of the anthropologist E. B. Tylor and others who followed the same general direction of interests. I will then consider the views of Durkheim, the Polish anthropologist Bronislaw Malinowski and of some later writers, especially the American sociologist Talcott Parsons. The latter's perceptive treatment of the main issues will serve as a guiding thread throughout the argument. But although his discussion is most helpful, he arrives at a position held by a number of earlier writers in this field which, in my opinion, places too much weight on the usefulness of the distinction between the sacred and the profane, a deceptively simple dichotomy that has had a distracting effect on the development of a comparative sociology of magico-religious institutions. But before elaborating this statement, let us return to the beginning.

When Tylor writes of the cult of the dead as central to the development of religion, his meaning is clear because he puts forward a minimal definition of religion, the belief in Spiritual Beings, that is, animism. This formulation was attacked from two main directions. In the first place, early reports of the beliefs of non-literate peoples described concepts pertaining to mystical forces of a non-personalized kind; typical of these were the *mana* of Melanesia and the *wakan* of the Dakota. The anthropologist R. R. Marett pointed to the similarities between these ideas, which he referred to as animatism, and the animistic beliefs employed by Tylor as the *differentia* of religion. Although Marett regarded both animism and animatism as in themselves non-religious, regarding the addition of emotive factors as critical in this respect, his contribution had the effect of blurring the previous distinction between magic and religion and led to the adoption of compromise terms such as ritual, sacred, non-logical, or even magico-religious to designate the domain formerly occupied by the non-scientific elements in the tripartite division of the world of belief into magic, religion and science employed by the earlier writers.

While Marett worked from basically the same starting points as his colleagues, Tylor and Frazer, the second main objection came from a radically different direction. To the general aspects of Durkheim's thesis I shall return later. His specific criticism of Tylor's own definition relates to the question of Buddhism. Here, he claimed, was a set of practices and beliefs, usually considered to be one of the great world religions, and yet described by one authority as 'a frankly materialistic and atheistic interpretation of the universe'. To include this interpretation of Buddhism some alternative formulation had to be devised. Starting from a standpoint put forward by the theologian Robertson Smith, Durkheim developed the thesis that all peoples recognized a radical dichotomy of the universe into the sacred and the profane. In accordance with this proposition, he offered his famous definition of religion as 'a unified system of beliefs and practices relative to sacred things, that is to say, things set apart and forbidden — beliefs and practices which unite into one single moral community called a Church, all those who adhere to them'.[3]

There have been other attempts to define the sphere of religious phenomena, by reference, for example, to emotive criteria such as feelings of awe. But efforts to isolate specifically religious experiences in this way have proven of little value to investigators in other societies. Evans-Pritchard, for example, has written: 'Certainly one cannot speak of any specifically religious emotion for the Nuer'.[4] In general, those pragmatically concerned with such questions have tended to adopt either the inclusive approach proposed by Durkheim or else the exclusive definition offered by Tylor. One reason for this is that certain aspects of Marett's objections have received little support from subsequent writers, and not only because of his introduction of emotive criteria. Malinowski, for example, has denied the relationship between magic on the one hand and animistic beliefs of the *mana* variety on the other. In support of his argument he quotes a Dakota text to the effect that 'all life is *wakan*' and contrasts this 'crude metaphysical concept' with the more specific attributes of Melanesian magic … 'there is little in common between the concepts of the *mana* type and the special virtue of magical spell and rite'.[5] However, other writers have accepted Marett's perception of a continuum of personal and impersonal supernatural powers, and, unlike him, have included both these spheres in the domain of the religious. According to this view, Tylor's minimal definition would have to be reworded to run: 'a belief in spiritual [or supernatural] agencies'.

[3] Durkheim 1947: 47.   [4] Evans-Pritchard 1956: 312.
[5] Malinowski 1954: 77–8.

The main dificulty here is in distinguishing between supernatural and natural, or spiritual and non-spiritual agencies. With 'beings' conceived as concrete entities on the human model, the distinction is possible to handle. But in dealing with non-human agencies and mystical powers, it is in many cases difficult to say whether the concepts are more akin to the physicist's force or to the Bergsonian *élan vital*. Or again the concept may span both the pragmatic-scientific and the philosophical-religious poles of meaning –

> The force that through the green fuse drives the flower
> Drives my green age;
> That blasts the roots of trees
> Is my destroyer.
>
> (Dylan Thomas)

An example of such an undifferentiated concept is the LoDagaa notion of 'medicine', *tĩĩ*, which has its counterpart in many other African societies. The term is used as readily for European medicines which have an empirical effect as for other concoctions such as love-potions which do not; it is applied to many different types of powder and includes gunpowder as well as the dried roots eaten to enable the hunter to shoot straight and true.

Of the two main definitions of religion which we have noted, the exclusive and the inclusive, it is the latter which has had the wider circulation. For it is implied by Marett's thesis, explicitly proposed by Durkheim and subsequently incorporated in the work of Radcliffe-Brown and his pupils, which has been a major contribution to the comparative study of religious phenomena. Another effective source of diffusion was the writings of Talcott Parsons, who utilized this definition as a basic reference point in his analytic schema. I shall therefore begin by considering the implications of adopting the extensive viewpoint as developed by Durkheim, paying particular attention to its implications for the study of the practices and beliefs associated with death.

Durkheim's own definition contains two elements: religion consists of beliefs and practices relative to sacred as distinct from profane things. But so, he says, does magic. To distinguish between these two spheres he introduced a second criterion; here he relied on Robertson Smith who had said that magic is opposed to religion as the individual to the social. Religion is public and has a church, whereas the magician has only his clientele, never a congregation. The contrast between the individual practitioner with particularized relations to his clients, a primitive doctor working with his 'bastard science', and the sacerdotal leader, the master of ceremonies, is one of some importance in the analysis of many social systems. But the distinction between these private and public roles, though related to other facets of religion and magic, offers a less than adequate focus for the definition of religious phenomena. Indeed, in an excellent discussion of this problem in relation to the Murngin material of northern Australia, Warner notes that magic too has its church, in that the effects of both good and bad magic depend to a considerable extent upon the commitment of the clients to a belief in the efficacy of the procedures they employ.[6] Consequently, the magician and his clientele also constitute a certain kind of moral community, which though not as explicit as in public ceremonials may be both morphologically and functionally very similar.

When Durkheim maintains that magic has no church, he means that it does not bind people together in the same way as do religious ceremonies; and the epitome of solidary procedures he sees in the *physical* assembling of the members of the group, i.e. in mass ceremonials. It is of course true that assemblies of this kind may and do play an important part in reaffirming certain of the central institutions of a society; this is the case with coronation services, with Red Army parades and with July 14th celebrations. Nevertheless, in making this the differentiating feature of religious action, Durkheim is tending to fall into the same error which confuses his early treatment of the problem of the individual and society. Initially at least he appears to confuse two sorts of distinction, on the one hand that between society as a collectivity of human beings and the individual as a single human entity, on the other that between society as the social element within the human personality and the individual as the organic or instinctual element. Eventually he settled for the latter distinction,[7] but not before he had sown the seeds of confusion

---

[6] Warner 1937: ch. 8.

[7] '... man is double. There are two beings in him: an individual being which has its foundation in the organism ... and a social being which represents the highest reality in the intellectual and moral order that we can know by observation – I mean society' (Durkheim 1947: 16).

for future readers. In defining religious phenomena, he concentrates once again upon the fact of the group assembling or, as some social anthropologists would use the term, its corporate features.[8] At one time he remarks that the reason for a group getting together is relatively unimportant compared with the fact of its assembling.

But it is one thing to stress the importance of convening groups – the two meanings of convention, an assembly and a custom, are not accidental. It is yet another to equate such groups with 'moral communities', as Durkheim tends at times to do; a congregation may be less 'solidary' and therefore less 'moral' for being dispersed, but as Warner's comments show, the existence of common norms, which is surely the only possible interpretation of the phrase 'a moral community', does not necessarily depend upon the existence of general assemblies. To make such an assumption is to fall into the same error as Durkheim does in his reference to Robertson Smith,[9] namely, that of confusing the public and the social. Although in any particular society there may be a great turnover in magical procedures, indeed the combination of an empirical end and a non-empirical means makes this to some extent inevitable, magic is no less a social phenomenon, in the strict sense, than is religion. Sorcery, for example, depends for its effects upon a certain degree of consensus, upon the acceptance of a set of social norms by a significant proportion of the members of a society. Though in one sense 'anti-social', it is pre-eminently 'social' in another, for the persistence of the belief in the attainment of pragmatic ends by non-empirical means depends entirely upon non-environmental factors; there is no direct reinforcement in the external, extra-human world.

---

[8] Neither Maine nor Weber introduces the criterion of assembling as a requisite of a corporate group. Neither does Radcliffe-Brown in his 1935 essay on 'Patrilineal and matrilineal succession' (reprinted in Radcliffe-Brown 1952). But subsequently he appears to consider this as an essential characteristic (1950: 41). Durkheim's influence is in evidence here. I regard this usage as making for possible confusions and prefer to speak of corporate groups in Radcliffe-Brown's earliest sense, i.e. in the legal sense of having an estate. It is also important at times to distinguish groups in which the members gather together for various purposes; these I speak of as 'assembling or convening groups'. Weber's *Verband* has also been translated 'corporate group', but he is referring to cases where the 'order is enforced by the action of specific individuals whose regular function this is, of a chief or "head" (*Leiter*), and usually also an administrative staff' (1947: 145–6). These are groups with a hierarchical authority system converging upon one or a few individuals; I refer to them as 'pyramidal groups', following the usage of Fortes and Evans-Pritchard (1940: 1–23).

[9] Durkheim 1947: 45, n. ii.

The tendency to embody the criterion of simultaneous face-to-face interaction in the concept of social groups in general and of religious groups in particular gives rise to certain inevitable difficulties, which Durkheim himself partly foresaw. He had to give special consideration to the position of beliefs in a personal destiny, cults of guardian spirits and other non-assembling forms of 'supernaturalism'. His treatment of these is not altogether happy, and as a consequence specialists in the religion of American Indians such as Radin, Lowie and Goldenweiser were led to undervalue his overall contribution to the study of religion. In reaction to his formulation of the problem, they followed Marett in trying to establish various emotive criteria of religious phenomena, a procedure which subsequent investigators have found of little value. What Durkheim did was to admit these 'private' cults as truly religious phenomena, but only by relating them to some more inclusive religious system. So the individual cults are seen solely in the context of the collective cult or church, and a church he tended to think of not only as the members of a faith, the congregation, but as a group assembling together in one place, the congregation physically united into one body. While these large-scale, face-to-face relations are of great importance, especially with regard to the effervescence which Durkheim associated with religious activities, they are neither the only sort of social relationship to produce this type of solidarity, nor can they be satisfactorily identified with religious activities as such, with sacred procedures in general. Indeed, what Durkheim is talking about in most of his analysis in *The Elementary Forms of the Religious Life* can more precisely be called *ceremonial*. Not infrequently he allocates to religion the functions and properties which might more properly be assigned to a phenomenon of greater generality, mass ceremonial.

Up to this point I have been considering the adequacy of the criteria Durkheim employed to distinguish religion from magic, namely its association with a church in the sense of a moral community. I now want to turn to the way in which he attempted to differentiate the whole sphere of magico-religious acts and beliefs by reference to the dichotomy between the sacred and the profane. This sphere is the one referred to by Radcliffe-Brown as 'ritual',[10] a term upon which it

---

[10] Radcliffe-Brown 1952.

is necessary to offer an explanatory comment. Generally the term has been used to refer to the action as distinct from the belief component of magico-religious phenomena. But the word is also employed in an attempt to avoid the distinction made by earlier writers between magic and religion. We have seen that for Durkheim religious rites are obligatory within a religious society of a church, while magical rites are optional. To fail in the observance of the one is sinful, while to omit magical rites is to incur only bad luck. As far as Malinowski was concerned, a magical rite has a definite practical purpose which is known to all who practise it and can be easily elicited from any native informant, while a rite is religious if it is simply expressive and has no particular purpose, being not a means to an end but an end in itself. This is the basis of Parsons' classification of rituals as 'religious in so far as the goal sought is non-empirical, magical, so far as it is empirical'.[11]

While not denying the possible theoretical interest of these and other differentiations between magical and religious activities, in his paper on 'Taboo'[12] Radcliffe-Brown tries to avoid the ambiguities involved by employing the term 'ritual' to cover magico-religious phenomena in general.[13] Thus he speaks of 'ritual values' in addition to ritual actions.

It is the entire compass of ritual or magico-religious activities which Durkheim associates with the sacred as distinct from the profane, a dichotomy which he describes in the following way: 'All known religious beliefs, whether simple or complex, present one common characteristic: they presuppose a classification of all things, real and ideal, of which men think, into two classes or opposed groups, generally designated by two distinct terms which are translated well enough by the words *profane* and *sacred*.'[14] This classification is in all aspects a relative one. 'The circle of sacred objects cannot be determined, then, once for all. Its extent varies infinitely, according to the different religions.'[15]

It is important to note that Durkheim conceives the sacred–profane dichotomy to exist within the actor frame of reference; he claims to be dealing with concepts which are actually present in all

[11] Parsons 1951: 375.   [12] Radcliffe-Brown 1939, reprinted in 1952.
[13] Radcliffe-Brown 1952: 136–9.   [14] Durkheim 1947: 37.
[15] Durkheim 1947: 37.

cultures, which are meaningful to the people themselves. It is for this reason that his definition plays such a central role in Parsons' valuable discussion of the theoretical convergences in the sociology of religion. One of the most important aspects of this development is the agreement that 'situations must be subjectively defined, and the goals and values to which action is oriented must he congruent with these definitions, must, that is, have "meaning"'.[16] Parsons sees this position as consistent not only with Weber's view of understanding (*Verstehen*) in the social sciences, but also with Malinowski's claim that the inhabitants of the Trobriand Islands recognize the distinction between technological, magical and religious acts. Indeed, he considers Tylor and Frazer as part of the same line of intellectual development because the 'rationalistic variety of positivism' was marked by 'the tendency to treat the actor as if he were a rational, scientific investigator, acting "reasonably", in the light of the knowledge available to him'.[17] While it is true that Tylor and Frazer rightly or wrongly attributed an intellectualist origin to religion, this was surely the result of their devotion to the categories and ways of thinking current in European society in the late nineteenth century rather than an adoption of the actor point of view of the 'other', to which they had access only through the reports of missionaries and travellers. However this may be, it is clear that their point of departure was less relative than that of Durkheim, whose one fixed point is the universal 'duality of the two kingdoms' of the sacred and the profane.

But let us turn to the empirical evidence and ask whether the dichotomy is in fact a universal or even a recurrent feature of the actor frame of reference. For although Durkheim so phrased his argument that the discovery of any society which did not recognize the division could be used in refutation, just as he employed Buddhism to reject Tylor's minimal definition of religion, we are not here concerned with the question of the universality of the phenomena as much as with the elucidation of useful analytic concepts. A major difficulty immediately presents itself. If the dichotomy is really as relative as Durkheim maintains when he speaks of infinite variations, then it is clearly not easy to decide what to look for. Many of the writers who have adopted this approach equate the profane and the sacred with

[16] Parsons 1954: 209–10.   [17] Parsons 1954: 199.

'normal' on the one hand, and with 'things set apart and forbidden' on the other, as Durkheim did in his original definition. But does not this take us far outside the bounds of the admittedly religious, to use Jane Harrison's phrase? In the absence of objective criteria might we not equally well fix upon *any* dichotomy a particular people make, 'good' and 'bad', 'black' and 'white', 'day' and 'night', and declare that this constitutes the equivalent of sacred and profane?

The empirical difficulties may be illustrated from two major discussions of this problem, which treat data on a particular society in the context of general theory. I refer to Malinowski's examination of Trobriand magic and to Evans-Pritchard's account of Azande witchcraft. In Parsons' delineation of the main trends in the sociology of religion, Malinowski is of crucial importance as demonstrating the existence, within the actor frame of reference, of the dichotomy between ritual and non-ritual phenomena in the context of fishing activities. His comment runs as follows:

Side by side with this system of rational knowledge and technique, however, and specifically not confused with it, was a system of magical beliefs and practices. These beliefs concerned the possible intervention in the situation of forces and entities which are 'supernatural' in the sense that they are not from our point of view objects of empirical observation and experience, but rather what Pareto would call 'imaginary' entities with a specifically sacred character.

Parsons concludes that 'this approach to the analysis of primitive magic enabled Malinowski clearly to refute both the view of Lévy-Bruhl, that primitive man confuses the realm of the supernatural and the sacred with the utilitarian and the rational, and also the view which had been classically put forward by Frazer that magic was essentially primitive science, serving the same fundamental functions'.[18] Malinowski, however, though he certainly maintained that magical acts were recognized as such by the society, did not feel he had rejected Frazer in his first report. Of the terms magic and religion, he writes in *Argonauts of the Western Pacific* 'although I started my field work convinced that the theories of religion and magic expounded in *The Golden Bough* are inadequate, I was forced by all my observations in New Guinea to come over to Frazer's position'.[19]

[18] Parsons 1954: 202–3.   [19] Malinowski 1922: 73n.

The difficulties of reconciling this acceptance of Frazer, for whom magic was bastard science, with a use of Durkheim's dichotomy, in which magic falls within the realm of the sacred, make the reader wonder what Malinowski means when he asserts that the Trobriand Islanders themselves recognize a distinction between the world of the sacred and the world of the profane. In the above quotation, Parsons, I think rightly, interprets this as a recognition of the distinction between the realm of the supernatural on the one hand and the utilitarian and the rational on the other. But that this is far from a universal distinction in non-literate societies is illustrated by the most comprehensive account we have which bears on this particular problem, namely Evans-Pritchard's treatment of Azande witchcraft.[20] Here the author accepts for heuristic purposes the distinction between 'ritual and empirical actions by reference to their objective results and the notions associated with them'.[21] But he emphasizes the difficulties raised by this acceptance:

Even by the definition of 'magical' and 'empirical' adhered to in this book it is not always easy to classify a simple act as one or the other. A man burns a piece of bark-cloth and, holding some magical plant in one hand, blows the smoke into the opening through which termites come out of their mounds when they swarm after rain. This is said to encourage them to come out. Azande say that the bark-cloth is termite-medicine, but they are probably speaking metaphorically.[22]

Again:

Azande offer the same explanation of a 'soul' acting to produce certain results in those technological activities in which there is a similar gap between action and result to the gap in magical techniques, a gap where nothing can be seen of what is happening – e.g., it is the 'soul' of the eleusine which accounts for the gap between planting of the seed and its germination and appearance above the ground.[23]

Evans-Pritchard denies that the Azande make the supernatural–natural distinction in the European sense, and there appears to be no confirmation of Malinowski's claim that the Trobriand Islanders make the same distinction as Europeans between technological and ritual acts. In Evans-Pritchard's discussion of leechcraft the lack of

[20] Evans-Pritchard 1937.   [21] Evans-Pritchard 1937: 463.
[22] Evans-Pritchard 1937: 464.   [23] Evans-Pritchard 1937: 464.

correspondence is evident; 'natural' and 'supernatural' forces as we conceive them are inextricably intertwined.[24] 'In every primitive community, studied by trustworthy and competent observers,' writes Malinowski, 'there have been found two clearly distinguishable domains, the Sacred and the Profane; in other words, the domain of Magic and Religion and that of Science'.[25] But it would seem from the Azande material that this is not the case; whatever differing attitudes exist towards the poles of technological and ritual activities as we see them, there is insufficient evidence to establish a universal conception of 'two clearly distinguishable domains'. When Malinowski declared that Trobriand Islanders clearly differentiated the magical from the technological aspects of canoe-building, he seems to have meant that they make a distinction between the situations in which they employ a certain type of verbal formula we would call a spell and those situations in which they do not. This is quite a different sort of distinction.

What Evans-Pritchard reports for the Azande holds equally well for the LoDagaa of northern Ghana. Among these people, there is no recognized distinction between the natural and the supernatural and, as Durkheim himself noted, this seems to be the case for most cultures. But neither do the LoDagaa appear to have any concepts at all equivalent to the vaguer and not unrelated dichotomy between the sacred and the profane which Durkheim regarded as universal. However, although the absence of correspondences in the cultural equipment of the people themselves weakens Durkheim's case, and has significant implications for certain aspects of Parsons' action schema, it does not necessarily destroy the utility of these categories as analytic tools if it proves possible to isolate objective criteria for their use. Can this be done?

Caillois begins his book, *Man and the Sacred*,[26] with the words: 'Basically, with regard to the sacred in general, the only thing that can be validly asserted is contained in the very definition of the term – that it is opposed to the profane.'[27] It is an indication of the extent to which the dichotomy has been uncritically adopted that a more recent writer on comparative religion, who takes the subject of

[24] Evans-Pritchard 1937: 478–510.   [25] Malinowski 1954: 17.
[26] Caillois 1939.   [27] Caillois 1959: 13.

his study to be 'hierophanies' or manifestations of the sacred, starts by quoting this remark with apparent approval.[28] Adequate as this may be for theological purposes, it is hardly sufficient as an analytic tool of comparative sociology. And Durkheim himself, despite his statement concerning infinite variations, offers something more concrete than this. Parsons notes that, negative features apart, Durkheim introduces two positive characteristics of 'ritual', that is, of acts oriented to sacred things. Firstly, there is 'the attitude of respect … employed as the basic criterion of sacredness throughout'. Secondly, 'the means–end relationship is symbolic, not intrinsic'.[29] Although 'respect' is often required by performances of a religious or ceremonial kind, it is by no means an invariant feature of such activities. Moreover, such an attitude is perhaps equally characteristic of authority relationships within the family, which could be designated 'sacred' only by an overly loose interpretation. The second criterion, the symbolic rather than intrinsic nature of the means–end relationship, is no less problematical. The first question that arises in any discussion of symbolic relationships is the level of analysis on which one is operating. Considerable confusion is caused by the failure to be clear as to whether a certain act or object is symbolic for the actor, or for the observer, or for both. In Parsons' schema, the symbolic relationship should exist within the actor frame of reference. But when it comes to dealing with the symbolic nature of ritual, the actor frame of reference is partly set on one side and the method of interpretation is likened to that of the psychoanalyst.[30] In other words, the reference of the sign is necessarily hidden from the actor.[31] This would also appear to be true of the Durkheimian formulation, according to which the symbolic reference of ritual, anyhow religious ritual, is 'society' or, in Parsons' explanatory phrase, 'the common ultimate-value attitudes which constitute the specifically "social" normative element in concrete society'.[32]

Radcliffe-Brown, whose views on this question derive from Durkheim, writes in a similar vein of the symbolic nature of what he

---

[28] Eliade 1958: xii.   [29] Durkheim 1947: 430–1.
[30] Durkheim 1947: 419 n. i.
[31] Ernest Jones writes of the symbol in the Freudian sense: 'the individual has no notion of its meaning, and rejects often with repugnance, the interpretation' offered of it ('The theory of symbolism', *British Journal of Psychology* 9 (1917–19), 184 quoted by Morris 1946: 276).
[32] Parsons 1954: 433–4.

calls 'ritual acts': '… ritual acts differ from technical acts in having in all instances some expressive or symbolic element in them'.[33] The term symbolic is explained in the following way: 'Whatever has a meaning is a symbol and the meaning is whatever is expressed by the symbol.' For Radcliffe-Brown the meaning of a rite is variously come by. At times the determination of meaning comes close to the attribution of social effects or social function, and the present passage continues: 'the method … I have found most profitable during work extending over more than thirty years is to study rites as symbolic expressions and to seek to discover their social functions'.[34] On other occasions the symbolic referent is the 'social structure, i.e. the network of social relations …';[35] at others, objects and actions of social importance.[36] At times he speaks of meaning being determined by the system of ideas with which a rite is associated.

The formulations of Parsons and Radcliffe-Brown are not identical, but both are agreed that ritual is essentially expressive or symbolic in nature. And in each case the interpreter of the symbolic relationship turns out to be the observer rather than the actor. In fact Radcliffe-Brown specifically rejects the explanation of ritual in terms of the conscious purposes of the participants; meaning is not to be found on the surface, though he claims rather lamely that 'there is a sense

---

[33] Radcliffe-Brown 1952: 143.   [34] Radcliffe-Brown 1952: 145.
[35] Radcliffe-Brown 1952: 144.
[36] In the introduction to the second edition of *The Andaman Islanders* (1933), Radcliffe-Brown distinguishes between what he sees as two interrelated concepts, *meaning* and *function*. The *meaning* of a rite 'lies in what it expresses, and this is determined by its associations within a system of ideas sentiments and mental attitudes' (viii). The notion of *function* 'rests on the conception of culture as an adaptive mechanism…' (ix) and concerns the contribution of the part to the continuity of the whole. Although he makes this distinction, he also remarks that 'In the two theoretical chapters of this book the discussion of meanings and the discussion of function are carried on together. Perhaps it would have been an advantage to separate them' (x). But in his later essay on 'Taboo', the Frazer lecture for 1939, the two also tend to get treated together. For instance, in his discussion of 'the meaning and social function' of the Andaman practice of avoiding the use of a person's name, the two operations are dealt with as one (1952: 146) and the custom is seen as a 'symbolic recognition' that the particular person is occupying an abnormal social position. In other words, the rite symbolizes an aspect of the 'social structure'. Again, both the meaning and social function of totemic rites are related to 'the whole body of cosmological ideas of which each rite is a partial expression' (1952: 145); here the rite is held to express the cosmology, and the cosmology in turn has a 'very special' relationship with the social structure. On the other hand, in his analysis of Andaman food taboos, the referent of ritual is seen as objects and customs of social importance, those imbued with 'ritual value'.

in which people always know the meaning of their own symbols, but they do so intuitively and can rarely express their understanding in words'.[37] As he himself realizes, once this fact is recognized the attribution of meaning or social function to a ritual raises serious problems of evidence. As for the determination of meaning with reference to ultimate values, the situation is even less clear. What are usually referred to as 'values' by social scientists are not the specific *desiderata* evinced by members of a society in their actions or in their beliefs. They are not what one philosopher, R. B. Perry, meant by 'any object of any interest', nor another philosopher, Charles Morris, by 'preferential behaviour', but high-level abstractions from such observational data. While writers like Parsons and the anthropologist Clyde Kluckhohn concentrate upon what they call 'value-orientations' rather than 'values', a yet more abstract concept. The difficulties involved are brought out when the sociologists Parsons and Shils define the related pattern variable concept as 'a dichotomy, one side of which must be chosen by an actor before the meaning of a situation is determinate for him, and thus before he can act with respect to that situation'.[38] It is difficult to see how this can be so when the actual list of pattern variables is examined; for example, the alternatives of specificity-diffuseness, useful as they may be to the sociologist involved in categorizing preferential behaviour, hardly represent concrete choices in the life of an Iowan farmer, let alone a Fulani herdsman to whom the formulation of such concepts would present problems of much greater complexity. Indeed, Kluckhohn in the same volume admits that the schemes put forward by Parsons and Shils, by F. Kluckhohn and by himself, are 'all analyses from an observer's point of view and with a minimum of content'.[39] An essential preliminary step, he remarks, is to get the 'feel of the culture' from a careful reading of classical ethnographies. It might be added that, given the apparent divergencies in the sensory equipment of the investigators, even the process of getting the 'feel' of a culture contains such a number of imponderables that the wary may well be daunted from proceeding to this further degree of abstraction.

The contention of Parsons that the symbolic reference of religious ritual is the common ultimate-value attitudes of a society appears to

---

[37] Radcliffe-Brown 1952: 143.   [38] Parsons and Shils 1952: 77.   [39] Kluckhohn 1952: 420–1.

lie behind the attempt of some anthropologists and sociologists to use Tillich's definition of religion as 'man's attitudes and actions with respect to his ultimate concern'. For example, Bellah, in his analysis of Tokugawa religion, writes:

This ultimate concern has to do with what is ultimately valuable and meaningful, what we might call ultimate value; and with the ultimate threats to value and meaning, what we might call ultimate frustration. It is one of the social functions of religion to provide a meaningful set of ultimate values on which the morality of a society can be based. Such values when institutionalized can be spoken of as the central values of a society.[40]

Lessa and Vogt have an identical starting point and make a similar comment: 'religion is concerned with the explanation and expression of the ultimate values of a society…'.[41] The utility of so vague and general a formulation is open to doubt. Quite apart from the question of the operation involved in specifying 'ultimate' or 'central' values, this definition would include all purely 'rational' pursuits in the economic or political sphere that were of major interest to the members of a particular society. Parsons himself notes that this definition diverges considerably from common usage; it is perhaps significant that in their pragmatic treatment of religious phenomena the above authors adhere much more closely to the 'traditional' sphere of discourse.

As the positive *differentia* of sacred acts, those acts which according to Durkheim define the sphere of religion, appear inadequate for our purpose, let us examine what Parsons calls the negative criterion of the definition, namely, the assumption that this category of practices is one which falls outside the intrinsic means–end schema. The means–end schema is intrinsic, according to Parsons, when the means brings about the end by processes of scientifically understandable causation. By 'falling outside the intrinsic means–end schema', Parsons does not merely intend to imply, as the nineteenth-century rationalists did, that such beliefs and practices were automatically 'irrational'. He recognizes a third type of action which is neither rational nor irrational (or pseudorational), but non-rational, or 'transcendental'; that is, it has no pragmatic end other than the very performance of the acts themselves, and cannot therefore be said either to have achieved, or

---

[40] Bellah 1957: 6.   [41] Lessa and Vogt 1958: 1.

not to have achieved, such an end. This tripartite distinction follows Pareto's classification of social action into (1) acts which meet 'logico-experimental' standards, (2) acts based on 'pseudo-scientific' theories either through ignorance or through error, (3) acts based upon 'theories which surpass experience'.[42] It is within this last category, he holds, that religious practices fall.

Parsons sees this classification as falling within the actor's own frame of reference; it refers, he writes, to 'the cognitive patterns in terms [of] which the actor is oriented to his situation of action'.[43] However, we have already seen that the testimony of a number of expert observers contradicts the view that all non-European societies normally make a distinction of this kind between transcendental and pseudo-scientific theories. If we accept this other view, then neither the negative nor the positive criteria of the 'sacred', as employed by Durkheim, constitute a real departure from the distinction made by the nineteenth-century rationalists between science, magic and religion. In this perspective, the search for universal categories corresponding to the sacred and the profane appears as an unsuccessful attempt to break loose from the earlier position, unsuccessful because of the difficulties involved in taking categories which are ultimately defined by reference to logico-experimental methods and trying to find their equivalents in non-literate societies.

The point I am making was seen by the anthropologist Nadel in his study, *Nupe Religion*. There he writes that we have to 'judge the transcendentality of things by our own way of thinking';[44] the separation of the natural from the supernatural can have a precise meaning only in our own system of thought. Indeed, as he rightly observes, 'the very conflict between supernatural and empirical knowledge on which we base our judgements is likely to be absent in a primitive culture'.[45] Evans-Pritchard provides evidence that this is so among the Azande and also maintains that the separation into natural and supernatural worlds is not to be found in Nuer thought. Among the LoDagaa too, as I have remarked, the spheres of the technological and the mystical are not clearly differentiated, either in terms of the ends sought or of the means employed.

---

[42] Parsons 1937: 429ff.   [43] Parsons 1954: 200.   [44] Nadel 1954: 3.
[45] Nadel 1954: 4.

The implications of this argument run counter to the Weberian insistence on *Verstehen* analysis in the social sciences, analysis in terms of the subjective aspect of action, its meaning to the participants themselves.[46] Indeed, Nadel himself feels uncomfortable at this discrepancy and hastens to assert, like Durkheim in similar circumstances,[47] that while simple societies do not dichotomize in the same way as we do, in terms of credibility, nevertheless they do differentiate between empirical and transcendental. The evidence for this, he declares, must be linguistic. But having delineated a Nupe dichotomy between 'knowledge' (*kpeyé*) and 'ritual' (*kuti*), he then undermines his own position by the *caveat* that: 'It is probably futile to expect that the native language should always provide precise distinctions of the kind we require, words like "normal" and "non-normal", "miraculous" or "superhuman", "sacred" and "profane".'[48]

So far this chapter has been devoted to a critical examination of existing usage of the concepts of religion and ritual, particularly as developed by Durkheim and those who have followed him. Before attempting to suggest more concrete ways of employing what have become vague, generalized and ambiguous terms, let me recapitulate the argument so far. I have been primarily concerned to reject Durkheim's assumption that the sacred–profane dichotomy is a universal feature of people's views of the human situation. The acceptance of this contrary standpoint means that it is no sounder for the observer to found his or her categorization of religious activity upon the universal perception by humanity of a sacred world any more than upon the actor's division of the universe into natural and supernatural spheres, a contention which Durkheim had himself dismissed. The enquirer into the field of religious behaviour is therefore placed in the same dilemma as the student of political institutions. In Western European society we perceive, and participate in, certain organizations which are labelled political, economic, educational, and so forth. In non-European societies the organizations are usually less differentiated; one single system of social groups may perform a greater variety of functions and the observer is then faced with the problem of stating which of the institutionalized activities carried

---

[46] The strains involved in attempting to confine sociological analysis to 'purposive' action are brought out in Dorothy Emmet's discussion of Nadel and Parsons (1958: 108).

[47] Durkheim 1947: 26.   [48] Nadel 1954: 6.

out by these latter correspond to those characterizing the differentiated organizations of advanced societies. In other words, he or she is forced to develop analytic tools out of our own folk-categories. In so doing the observer has an obligation to respect both our own folk-categories, which form the basis of his or her analytic concepts, and the folk-categories of the actors themselves, which provide the raw material to which this conceptual apparatus is applied. On the other hand, the observer cannot be required to limit him- or herself to 'meaning' as the actor him- or herself perceives it, that is, to the folk-categories of the people he or she is studying. Indeed, it is difficult to see how those who maintain the contrary view could carry the full implications of their standpoint into the treatment of specific sociological data. A philosopher who starts from an acceptance of the Weberian doctrine of *Verstehen*, and but a limited acquaintance with the more empirical contributions of social science, has argued that all sociology is impossible since the observer can never get outside the conceptual apparatus of his or her own society nor, conversely, inside that of any other.[49] This is not an illegitimate conclusion, given the Weberian premise. But it implies the unacceptability of that premise in its literal form.

To demonstrate that the sacred–profane dichotomy is not a universal feature of the actor's situation is not of course to render it unserviceable as an analytic tool. In order to determine its possible utility for such purposes, I then examined the criteria of sacredness. Of the two positive features, respect and the symbolic element, the first failed to indicate either a category or polar type of specifically religious relationships. While in the light of the essentially external character of the dichotomy, the attribution of a 'symbolic' or 'expressive' element to ritual or religious (i.e. 'non-rational') behaviour often turned out to be no more than a way of announcing that the observer is unable to make sense of an action in terms of an intrinsic means–end relationship, a 'rational' cause and effect nexus, and has therefore to assume that the action in question stands for something other than it appears to; in other words, that it expresses or is symbolic of something else.[50] But what is that something else?

---

[49] Winch 1958.
[50] Similar qualms were expressed by de Brosse in 1760 about allegorical interpretations of myths in his work, *Du culte des dieux fétiches*: 'l'allégorie est un instrument universel qui se

This is where the recognition of the external character of the sacred–profane, supernatural–natural dichotomy becomes important. For it points to the fact that the referent of the symbol is supplied by the observer, not the actor. What the former assumes is expressed (or symbolized) is his or her interpretation of 'society', 'ultimate values', 'social order' or the 'social structure'. I do not wish to imply that some magico-religious behaviour is not 'symbolic' from the actor's point of view. Clearly it is. But so is much other behaviour. Indeed, in the last analysis, all verbal behaviour is sign behaviour. Hence the category of symbolic action does not in itself mark off an area or polar type of social action which it is in any way possible to characterize as ritual or religious. For it can be said, in an important sense, that all social action is 'expressive' or 'symbolic' of the social structure, because the more general concept is simply an abstraction from the more specific. It is not, however, 'expressive' in the way many sociologists implicitly assume, that is, it does not express major principles of social behaviour. Indeed, such an approach simply involves the reification of an organizing abstraction into a causal factor.

What happens, then, is that symbolic acts are defined in opposition to rational acts and constitute a residual category to which 'meaning' is assigned by the observer in order to make sense of otherwise irrational, pseudo-rational or non-rational behaviour. And consequently the earlier conclusion reached by the examination of the positive criteria of ritual acts is reinforced by looking at the negative criterion, that is, the contention that these practices fall outside the intrinsic means–end schema. Once it is recognized that the accepted criteria for the isolation of sacred or ritual or magico-religious phenomena are derived not from the actor's but from the observer's assessment of what is intrinsic, certain problems in the study of comparative religion fall into place. The way is open for a partial rehabilitation of the usages of the nineteenth-century anthropologists.

The conclusion of this summary of the argument leads directly to the final portion of this chapter, which consists of an attempt to suggest more definite ways of using not only the concepts of 'religion'

prête à tout. Le système du sens figuré une fois admis, on y voit facilement tout ce que l'on veut comme dans les nuages: la matière n'est jamais embarrassante; il ne faut plus que de l'esprit et de l'imagination: c'est un vaste champ, fertile en explications, quelles que soient celles dont on peut avoir besoin' (6–7).

and 'ritual', but also that of 'ceremonial', for it is this, I have claimed, that Durkheim identifies with religious activity. To begin with 'religion', it is significant that in one of the most thoughtful contributions to the study of the religion of a non-literate people, Evans-Pritchard defined his field of discourse in Tylorian terms. With all its limitations this definition appears to offer the nearest approach to a resolution of our problem.

But the acceptance of Tylor's minimum definition still leaves unresolved Marett's problem concerning the boundary between spiritual beings and spiritual forces. While beliefs of this kind must inevitably fall along a continuum, the associated practices present the opportunity for a sharper discrimination. We may take as a point of departure Frazer's definition of religious acts in terms of the propitiation of supernatural powers. Acts of propitiation directed towards supernatural powers consist of sacrifice (food-offerings and especially blood sacrifice), libation (offerings of drink), gifts of non-consumable material objects, prayer (verbal offerings) and the 'payment of respect' by other forms of gesture. We may say then that religious beliefs are present when non-human agencies are propitiated on the human model. Religious activities include, of course, not only acts of propitiation themselves but all behaviour which has reference to the existence of these agencies. Such a formulation does not entirely dispose of Marett's savage shouting at the thunderstorm; indeed such acts, if fully institutionalized and related to a set of cosmological beliefs concerning spiritual beings, would certainly be considered as religious within the terms of our definition. But however imperfect the instrument may be, it does, I suggest, provide a focus for the comparative analysis of religious institutions which is of greater utility than the extensive definition preferred by Durkheim; indeed, it is the one employed in practice by the majority of writers in this field, whatever expressed theory they may have adopted.

With regard to 'ritual', I earlier called attention to the fact that Radcliffe-Brown and other writers used this term to designate the whole area of magico-religious acts and beliefs. In adopting such a usage, these writers followed Durkheim's rejection of the admittedly external, observer-imposed distinction of the nineteenth-century 'intellectualists', and accepted one based upon the sacred–profane dichotomy, which was assumed to lie within the actor's own definition of the situation. The conceptual difficulties involved in this usage have already been discussed. Of the alternative possibilities, one is to identify 'ritual' with the magico-religious in the sense meant by Tylor and Frazer. A problem arises here from the fact that, both in common usage and in sociological writings, the term is frequently given a wider significance. The *Oxford Dictionary*, for example, defines a rite as '(1) a formal procedure or act in a religious or other solemn observance; (2) the general or usual custom, habit, or practice of a country, class of persons, etc., now specifically in religion or worship'. Not unconnected with the idea of the formality of the procedure (e.g. in 'ritual intercourse') is the further implication that an act so described is either not directed to any pragmatic end ('rituals of the table') or, if so directed, will fail to achieve the intended aim ('fertility rituals'). Thus the term has often a wider reference than the field of magico-religious behaviour and 'rituals of eating' may or may not be connected with such beliefs. The point was recognized by Nadel when he wrote in his account of Nupe religion:

When we speak of 'ritual' we have in mind first of all actions exhibiting a striking or incongruous rigidity, that is, some conspicuous regularity not accounted for by the professed aims of the actions. Any type of behaviour may thus be said to turn into a 'ritual' when it is stylized or formalized, and made repetitive in that form. When we call a ritual 'religious' we further attribute to the action a particular manner of relating means to ends which we know to be inadequate by empirical standards, and which we commonly call irrational, mystical, or supernatural.[51]

For Nadel, the category 'ritual' is inclusive and relates to any type of excessively formal action, while religious ritual (and in this he includes magic) covers acts where the means–end relationship is deemed inadequate by empirical standards. This aspect of his distinction seems a little tenuous, as presumably if the means display an incongruous rigidity, they are also to some extent empirically inadequate. Moreover, this statement of the situation fails to take account of the view, explicitly developed by Pareto, that much magico-religious behaviour is non-rational rather than irrational. But with these qualifications, Nadel's position is basically similar to that taken in this chapter.

---

[51] Nadel 1954: 99.

What has been said concerning the 'secular' nature of much ritual is equally applicable to 'ceremonial'. Let us first explore the inter-relationship between the two concepts. The anthropologist Monica Wilson used them in the following way. Ritual she defines as 'a primarily religious action ... directed to securing the blessing of some mystical power ... Symbols and concepts are employed in rituals but are subordinated to practical ends'.[52] Ceremonial is an 'elaborate conventional form for the expression of feeling, not confined to religious occasions'. Here ritual is equated with religious action, while ceremonial is a more inclusive concept referring to any 'elaborate conventional form'. She perceives that it may be important not automatically to identify ceremonial with religious performances in the way that Durkheim had tended to do. For while ceremonials such as Corpus Christi Day processions, which celebrate mystical powers, may perform similar functions to those like the anniversary of the October Revolution, which have an exclusively secular significance, it is often useful to distinguish between them, particularly when considering the beliefs involved. However, it seems simpler to make the same distinction by using the term ritual in the general sense of what Wilson speaks of as 'conventional' action, while referring to the activities addressed to 'some mystical power' as religious. Following the formulation of Radcliffe-Brown, ceremonial may then be used to refer to those collective actions required by custom, performed on occasions of change in the social life. Thus a ceremonial consists of a specific sequence of ritual acts, performed in public.

In conclusion then, by ritual we refer to a category of standardized behaviour (custom) in which the relationship between the means and end is not 'intrinsic', i.e. is either irrational or non-rational. Within this general category falls magical action, which is essentially irrational, since it has a pragmatic end which its procedures fail to achieve, or achieve for other reasons than the patient, and possibly the practitioner, supposes. This is Frazer's 'bastard science'. Then there are religious acts, which may be irrational (as in the case of many forms of sacrifice and prayer) or they may be non-rational, as in many public celebrations, but all of which involve supernatural beings. Then finally there is a category of ritual which

---

[52] Wilson 1957: 9.

is neither religious nor magical; it neither assumes the existence of spiritual beings nor is it aimed at some empirical end, though this is not to deny that it may have a recognized 'purpose' within the actor frame of reference as well as some 'latent function' from the observer's standpoint. Within this category of ritual fall ceremonials of the non-magico-religious kind: civil marriage ceremonies, rituals of birth and death in secular households or societies. Here too are the acts that we cannot speak of as public ceremonials, the 'rituals of family living'[53] or 'rituals of liquidation'[54] and similar types of formalized interpersonal behaviour.

The intention of this chapter has been to examine the ranges of meaning assigned to certain basic concepts as used in some classical texts in the sociology of religion with a view to clarifying their use as analytic tools. The general conclusion is that it is impossible to escape from the fact that the category of magic religious acts and beliefs can be defined only by the observer and that attempts to see either this or the sacred–profane dichotomy as a universal part of the actor's perception of his or her situation are misleading. Any effectiveness which these terms may have in comparative studies depends upon a realization of their limitations and involves a return to the usages of earlier, pre-Durkheimian writers in this field, anyhow as a starting point for further exploration.

POSTSCRIPT

The first draft of this chapter was given in the early 1960s at a seminar in Oxford, and I would like to acknowledge the stimulus of a series of discussions with M. Richter, of Hunter College, New York. The chapter was rewritten when I was a fellow at the Center for Advanced Study in the Behavioral Sciences, 1959–60, but some additional comment upon more recent developments seemed called for.

When I first wrote, commitment to the sacred–profane, *ritus–mos* disinction dominated social anthropological thinking in the field of comparative religion. The influence of Durkheim is still much in evidence here, and nowhere more clearly than in the work of the anthropologist Lévi-Strauss, and those who have followed his theoretical

---

[53] Bossard and Boll 1950.   [54] Leites and Bernaut 1954.

interests. Another anthropologist, Edmund Leach, saw the distinction as referring to aspects rather than types of social action, and ritual as a 'pattern of symbols' referring to the 'system of socially approved "proper" relations between individuals and groups'.[55] Another anthropologist, Rodney Needham,[56] however, employed the radical dichotomy in much the same way as Durkheim and Lévi-Strauss when he commented upon the Italian anthropologist Bernardo Bernardi's material[57] on the Mugwe, the Failing Prophet of the Meru of Kenya. The emphasis which these writers give to this distinction is connected with their general interest in 'elementary structures' with two or three constituents ('binary' or 'tertiary structures'), a morphological scheme which divides all into conceptual dichotomies and trichotomies with an attractive neatness.[58] But apart from the more general criticism made in the body of the chapter, there are two further dangers here. Firstly, such radical distinctions are sometimes seen as having explanatory power in themselves, especially when an association is made between two or more sets of 'oppositions'. Secondly, just because the elucidation of such relationships is given an explanatory force, so there is a tendency to assume their presence on evidence of a rather slender kind.

The difficulties behind some aspects of Durkheim's position became clearer in the course of the next few years and this has led to a change of approach. In the chapter itself, I draw attention to Evans-Pritchard's adoption of the Tylorian definition of religion in his analysis of the Nuer.[59] In his introduction to the translation of the essays by the sociologist, Robert Hertz, an associate of Durkheim, he also rejects the polarity between the sacred and the profane which he finds, as I do, 'vague and ill-defined'.[60] The New Zealand anthropologist Raymond Firth, in his Huxley Memorial Lecture of 1959, calls upon anthropologists not to be afraid of subscribing to the 'intellectual, rationalist view' held by nineteenth-century writers in the field, and puts forward a definition of religion not far removed from that of Tylor. 'Religion', he writes, 'may be defined as a concern of man in society with basic human ends and standards of value, seen in relation to non-human entities, or powers.'[61] Moreover the

[55] Leach 1954: 15.   [56] Needham 1960.   [57] Bernardi 1959.
[58] e.g. Lévi-Strauss 1956, 99ff.   [59] Evans-Pritchard 1956.
[60] Evans-Pritchard 1960: 12.   [61] Firth 1959: 131.

conclusion which he reaches after examining Tikopian material upon spirit mediumship is broadly in line with Evans-Pritchard's account of Nuer religion, namely, that while some aspects of religious practices and beliefs are closely related to the 'social structure', others are relatively loosely linked and operate as 'semi-independent variables'.

To anyone outside the tradition of academic sociology, such a conclusion might well pass without comment. But a corollary of the immense impetus which Durkheim's great work, *The Elementary Forms of the Religious Life*, gave to the sociology of religion has been a tendency to over-determine the relationship of the religious with other social institutions. Moreover, definitions of ritual and religion as 'symbolic' of social relations have the disadvantage not only of being hampered by ambiguities involved in the term symbolic, but of seeming to assert as a general principle precisely what requires to be demonstrated in each particular case.

In the Frazer lecture for 1957, *The Context of Belief*,[62] the anthropologist Daryll Forde has called attention to other gaps in the Durkheimian approach, emphasizing in particular that other ritual practices such as the fetishism of the Yakö are not simply symbolic expressions of social relationships, but are also concerned with environmentally determined conditions, such as the incidence of disease. Here as elsewhere, he lays special emphasis upon the manipulative aspects of the 'supernatural economy',[63] a theme also pursued in my own discussion of the inevitable 'circulation of shrines' arising from the built-in obsolescence of those 'irrational' magico-religious agencies which make specific promises that they are later seen not to fulfil.[64] Some of the broader implications for the Durkheimian thesis had been brought out in Warner's examination of the Murngin material from Australia,[65] from which it is clear that the distinction between magic and religion on an instrumental–expressive basis (to use Parsons' terminology) is not viable. In his theoretical treatment of the subject, Goode[66] suggests a continuum, with magic in general more instrumental, religion more expressive. In an interesting article entitled 'A definition of religion, and its uses',[67] Horton has examined variations in religious behaviour along a similar axis, the

[62] Forde 1958a.   [63] Forde 1958b.   [64] Goody 1957.
[65] Warner 1937: ch. 8.   [66] Goode 1951.   [67] Horton 1960.

poles of which he specifies as manipulation and communion. His definition of religion is essentially that of Tylor's and the central argument is close to the one developed here, except that he is rather more sanguine than I am about the immediate profit to be gained from adopting such a position.

CHAPTER 2

Oral 'literature'

In this chapter, I shift from discussing general problems about the definition of religion, ritual and orality to a more specific area with 'myth' and other 'standardized oral forms', or what is often called 'oral literature'. Here I survey the different forms so that I can go on to analyse and criticize the material I (and my helpers) collected among the LoDagaa and elsewhere in northern Ghana. I argue that the context of recitation, especially the audience, has to be considered more seriously. By lumping all together, anthropologists and others have given equal weight to folktales as to 'myths', not realizing that the first are often specifically children's 'literature' and therefore cannot be taken as representative of adult thinking. 'Myths' again are seen as typical of oral cultures, and a genre which is transformed by the advent of writing, like many of the others. However, folktales, directed largely to children, also persist in the nurseries of written cultures.

Oral 'literature' was the standard form (or genre) found in societies without writing. The term is also used to describe the quite different tradition in written civilizations where certain genres are transmitted by word of mouth or are confined to the unlettered (the 'folk'). One is using 'literature' even of purely oral terms. Nevertheless, it is the best phrase available for describing these two usages, although they should often be distinguished. While certain forms such as the folktale continue to exist especially among the unlettered component of complex societies, what might also be called the 'oral tradition' (to indicate it is part of a wider constellation) is inevitably influenced by the elite, by written culture. The term 'literature' poses problems since it is ultimately derived from the Latin *littera*, 'letter', essentially a written, indeed alphabetic, concept. The phrases 'standardized oral

forms' and 'oral genres' have been suggested in place of oral literature, but, since the word literature is so widely used, it has to be
reckoned with, even though it is essential for any discussion to recall
the major differences between the two registers, oral and written, as
well as the way in which the latter influences the spoken word (in
what I will call the lecto-oral).

It seems right that I should say a little more about oral 'literature'.
The concept of literature in some societies is obviously 'anachronistic';
one cannot have literature without letters. But there are undoubtedly
certain forms of speech in oral cultures that are marked off from
dialogue, from monologue, from ordinary speech. There may well
be more of a boundary problem in some societies and one type of
these standardized oral forms may slide into another, may not be
distinguished from it, like romance and novel in English as distinct
from *roman* in French and the equivalent in Italian. It is possible
that myths and folktales may be so merged. But that does not mean
that we as observers cannot make a distinction, even if the cultures
do not. That involves the concept of 'genre'. Song is clearly marked
off. So too is a recitation like the Bagre since it occurs very much in
a special occasion. So for us does a folktale, even if it is 'composed'
by an adult (like J. K. Rowling) and used in some circumstances in
mythical recitals (as in the *Iliad*). But if not specially individualized
in the terminology, this speech is marked, as are prayers to the gods.
I refer to these types of speech as 'standardized oral forms', but 'oral
genres' would be as acceptable if it is remembered that the division
between them is mine, the anthropologist's, not necessarily referred
to by the 'actors' themselves. The term oral 'literature' is obviously
that of a person in a literate society looking for equivalents; these
existed in the shape of marked 'speech' of kinds that have a very wide
distribution, despite the general differences in character between
South America and Africa.

THE RELATION OF SPEECH TO WRITING

Since writing is always an additional register to speech, its advent has
necessarily had a profound influence on the latter, which is never the
same as when it stands alone. Writing's effects have been dramatic
on society generally, but, for much of the span of written recorded

history, writing and reading were confined to a small, elite minority of a population, with a large proportion of people continuing to depend on lecto-oral communication alone, especially in the sphere of 'literature'. In many cases these two traditions existed side by side. That situation creates problems for the analysis of the various genres, for there is a tendency today to read back the characteristics of literate literature (such as narrativity, that is, entailed sequence in storytelling, as in a novel) into purely oral genres. Written literature is never simply a matter of writing down what already exists; a myth or story is always changed in being 'transcribed' and takes its place among a set of new genres as well as among modifications of old ones.

The term 'folklore' generally refers to certain of the spoken (or non-written) activities of complex, literate cultures where only a minority can read and write and where the rest are unlettered, 'illiterate', a frequent situation of the peasantry in the post-Bronze Age cultures of Europe and Asia. While their activities have some links with parallel ones in purely oral cultures, they are inevitably influenced by the always-dominant literary modes, especially those related to the major (written) religions. The accounts in 'folklore' are largely confined to the realm of peripheral beliefs. But even the forms taken by genres such as the epic, characteristic of early cultures with writing, can influence folklore.

It is clear that, in societies with writing, a great deal of communication – including communication that eventually takes on an artistic, literary form – is still done by word of mouth. Not only is this an aspect of all human intercourse, but it was inevitably the case in every sphere until near-universal literacy was achieved in Europe during the last quarter of the nineteenth century. Until that time, literature had to be orally presented for the large part of the population. That did not mean this literature was uninfluenced by the written word; indeed, some of the oral communication consisted in the repetition of written texts, as when lessons from the Bible were preached to an unlettered populace. A written epic, as was the case with the Hindu Vedas or with the works of Homer, might be learned by heart and recited rather than read to the population at large, by the rhapsodes in the latter case and by the Brahmans in the former. Of course a society with writing might inherit some genres, such as folktales, largely unchanged from an earlier, purely oral culture, whereas other genres, such as the epic, would undergo a sea change.

Part of the influence of the written word on speech consisted in the development not of oratory, which was already practised, but of its formal counterpart, rhetoric, with an explicit body of written rules. In purely oral cultures, those specialists in the spoken word could achieve fame and be rewarded for their appearance in presenting a case at a moot or at a court. More directly in the field of the arts, specialist reciters, especially of praise songs but also of other lengthy recitations, might be recompensed for their contributions, either as freelance performers or as professionals. So too with early written forms, such as epics.

Many early written forms, such as the Breton lays, draw their subject matter from spoken genres, though inevitably transformations take place in the face of the new media. There has also been a good deal of exchange between coexistent folk and written (elite) literature. Homer's poems incorporated 'popular' tales, for example, as did the Anglo-Saxon *Beowulf*, although these transfers are as much between genres as between the registers of speech and writing; the process was akin to the taking up of popular melodies, such as the *bourrée* of rural France, by those composing elite music in the urban courts of seventeenth-century Europe.

THE EXAMPLE OF THE EPIC

The Homeric poems are often viewed as oral epics that have been transposed into writing. Commentators have dwelt on the presence of certain features such as the formulaic expressions (epithets and repeated verses) that they see as typical of oral forms. Yet, while the regular repetition of phrases is found in such forms, some have argued that the precise format of Homer's 'formula', as defined by the American scholar Milman Parry in comparing Homer with twentieth-century Yugoslav epics, is very likely an early literate device.

The epic itself is a prime example of how we wrongly impose the characteristics of a literate society onto a non-literate one. It is often assumed to be a typical product of oral cultures, being sung by professional bards at courts or in army camps. However, records of epics in purely oral cultures are sparse: in Africa, for example, they are rare, being present largely in the Sahara, where their existence appears to owe much to written Muslim cultures. Otherwise epics tend to be found in early states with important warrior classes that enjoy hearing of the brave exploits of their predecessors, like *Beowulf*. These societies already have writing, but the texts are often committed to memory and reproduced verbally by the speaker rather than read aloud, recited in gatherings of chiefs and warriors by specialist bards, in fact works that have been written down, like the *Odyssey*. Indeed, only because they have been written down are they known to us and could be memorized exactly by the ancient Greeks. It is a regular characteristic of early written works, such as Homer or the Vedas, that, although written versions exist, these are learned by heart, internalized and reproduced through the spoken word alone, just as is often the case with monotheistic religious texts like the Quran and the Bible. At the very moment in history when writing allows one to dispose of verbal memory as a means of recalling such works, the role of such memory is in fact enhanced – hence part of the difficulty in deciding whether these works are both orally composed and orally reproduced. They are certainly typical of societies where only the few can read and where mnemonic skills and devices that encourage the perfect oral reproduction of written texts are therefore encouraged.

The way that purely oral forms have been changed under the influence of written cultures is illustrated by the *Kalevala*, the Finnish national epic, a final version of which was published in 1849 by Elias Lönnrot. A systematic collector of folk poetry, Lönnrot concluded that what had been recorded as distinct poems could be conflated into a continuous folk epic. By joining a number of shorter compositions together with material of his own and imposing on the whole a unifying plot, he imposed the characteristics of literate, written literature onto the products of a supposedly oral culture. Its publication had an enormous influence on Finnish life. It has been suggested that the Gilgamesh epic (of the seventh-century BCE Akkadian-language tablets found at Nineveh) may have been constructed in a similar way; other cases have been reported from Africa. In North America stories that centre on particular characters such as Coyote or Raven are sometimes grouped together by scholars into cycles, but it seems doubtful whether these cycles represent a meaningful category of continuous performance for the Native Americans who created these tales. They may well be considered distinct.

Obvious differences between oral and written literatures exist for authorship and for the audience. In oral cultures the memory of authorship, though never entirely absent, is of little general importance – occasionally with songs but not with myths, folktales and, rarely, with epics (though these are features of early literate cultures). That is not to say that these genres do not become the subjects of intellectual property rights. Songs may be associated with particular clans, recitations with specific associations (such as the Bagre of the LoDagaa). But usually no individual author is traced. That absence, however, does not imply that there is a process of collective composition. Each reciter will introduce variations of his own, some of which will be taken up by succeeding speakers for whom the previous version will have been the (or a) model. In this way changes are constantly being introduced in an interlocking chain by individuals but anonymously, without looking back to any fixed original. Only with writing and with oral recitations in literate societies, as in the case of Homer or the Vedas, is it possible to refer the oral transmission to an original, partly because writing introduces a new dimension to verbal memory and partly because reference can then always be made back to the 'correct' version. As a result, it seems to be in these early literate societies that the strong development of mnemonic skills and aides-memoires is first found; these forms of assistance to memory are largely linked to writing, to 'visible speech'. In purely oral cultures, re-creation usually takes the place of a concern with exact recall.

ORAL GENRES

Apart from the epic, the main oral genres include the folktale; song, comprising laments, praise and work songs; folk drama; myth; and the closely related legend and historical recitation. All of these are discussed in detail below. In addition there are also the minor genres of the proverb and the riddle.

While these are not necessarily always given separate designations in local languages, in scholarly practice they are distinguished because of differences in their form, content and function, which relate partly to their audience. At the very broadest level, folktales are rarely seen as anything but fictional, whereas the other genres, apart from song, have quite a different relation to 'truth'. In purely oral societies, recitations and songs encompass the whole of life's experience, including cosmology and theology. But in early societies with writing, the religious domain tends to be incorporated by way of texts associated with a canon (its most important scriptural works), leaving oral literature to deal with the peripheral – with magic, charms and fairy tales. With any literature, it is important to consider not only the speaker but the audience and the situational context. Intention, form and content make all the difference between recitations in a religious or ritual ceremony and the kind of story told at a *veillée* (communal evening event) in Europe or at an equivalent gathering in Africa. These differences mean that to incorporate all these genres in one holistic analysis of a culture, symbolism, or myth means mixing levels of communication that are aimed at very different audiences. Some tales, for example, may specifically be directed at children (fairy tales), others at adults (myths), others to chiefs (dynastic histories); each genre has a different position in the total culture, with the first circulating more freely between cultures, the latter two being more closely linked to one or to adjacent ones.

FOLKTALES

Folktales are virtually universal, as Thompson and others have shown. These are short, occasionally in verse, sometimes with an ending that echoes the explanations embedded in Rudyard Kipling's *Just So Stories* (e.g. 'How the Camel Got His Hump'), possibly with an apparently irrelevant coda. The personages consist of humans, animals, gods and, more rarely, other 'inventions' such as giants and monsters, who interact with one another by speech and by gesture. In this wide array of tales there is a place for the salacious, and some stories are apparently directed specifically to adults (or at least to adolescents); but the bulk of folktales undoubtedly anticipate an audience of children. In Australia, as elsewhere, they were told by mothers to their young but also to tourists and anthropologists. Grim as are some of their contents, they are 'nursery or fairy tales', to use an English term equivalent to Charles Perrault's 'fairy stories' (*contes de fées*).

Because the vast proportion of folktales are intended for children, it is quite mistaken for anthropologists, who collect them avidly, to use them as evidence of the typical thoughts of primitive societies or for historians to do the same for the rural population of seventeenth-century Europe. Children's tales are for age-specific audiences and circulate widely across cultures, today as in the past; stories of the 'man in the moon' cannot be taken as indicative of adult belief, let alone of any particular society. But just such an approach is sometimes taken by those who see culture completely holistically, with each element having the same representative status and value in characterizing mentalities, beliefs and practices, and with each item taken to exist within an undifferentiated cultural ensemble of artistic forms. In fact, the relationship of these stories to other aspects of culture is very particular.

While their audience is of an age-specific and sometimes of a gender-specific kind, these stories also persist over long periods of time and have no very close relationship to a particular culture at a particular time: examples from English-speaking societies include children's rhymes and songs such as 'Ring a Ring of Roses' and 'Three Blind Mice' and the story 'Jack and the Beanstalk'. Like the rhyme 'Frères Jacques', the story of Cinderella (or the Nancy, that is, Ananse, or spider cycle in Asante or in the Caribbean), they cross socio-political and linguistic boundaries rather freely, making some adaptations as they do so through the mouths of individual story-tellers. Such movement across boundaries as between Africa and America, encouraged by the relatively small size of individual oral cultures, also involves the transposition of these stories into other dialects and even other languages, which emphasizes the transcultural character of their themes and expressions. The relative smallness of these cultures means inevitable transactions across boundaries, including often marriage and trade, so that people often speak more than one language; not only do fictional stories travel in the same way but other oral literature at times includes passages in more than one language. It is this comparative insulation of children's stories from specific cultural pressures that accounts for their relative homogeneity around the world, and also for their frequent use of non-human animals and pan-human themes. They are partly insulated because they are repeated by heart to children who are concerned with the continuity and rhythm of the words and with the pan-human theme rather than whether the bears have disappeared from the forest, let alone whether they can talk.

It is important to appreciate that cultures cannot be considered as wholes in every respect, that they often have ill-defined boundaries, and that their members are stratified by age, gender and class, with each level having its own preferred forms of literature. The novels of and characters within the Harry Potter series of the British author J. K. Rowling, for example, do not have the same significance for everyone, whether within one ethnic group or in others; on the other hand, children's stories in particular have a cross-national appeal. To adopt an entirely holistic approach, as is common in much cultural anthropology and in the social sciences more generally, is to infantilize the thought and practices of earlier generations and other cultures in unfortunate ways. Oral literature, like its written counterpart, is differentiated by audience in various ways. In non-literate societies, fiction is largely for children; adults gravitate to more 'serious' forms, such as myth and legend, though the role of play and entertainment in cultures such as the Navajo of America or the Bemba of Zambia should not be underestimated – playing with words, playing with sounds, playing with gestures.

Fables are a subcategory of folktale, employing animals as well as humans as the main characters. In the form they are known today, either from ancient Greece and Rome (e.g. Aesop's fables) or from India, they are in fact products of written cultures as parables are in the Bible, but are close in many respects to folktales more generally. But they are often allegorical, referring to moral issues. In fact allegory is a genre in itself, in which the listener is encouraged to look for hidden meanings beneath the literal surface, but this is more clearly a product of written culture where inspection is more deliberate and considered than is usually possible in oral culture.

SONGS AND SINGING

Song plays a very general role in oral culture. The words of a song often resemble lyric poetry in form, having to be of a tight metrical structure because of the musical accompaniment. Equally, when epic and other recitations are accompanied by a musical instrument or a strong beat, the rhythmic verbal structure is always influenced. An important variety of song is the lament at the death of an individual, which may take the form of stressed speech or follow a more melodic line.

Songs may be included in rituals as well as in folktales and other genres, but they are often performed solely for entertainment. The melodies themselves may be elaborated and expanded upon by way of musical instruments, leading to innumerable variations invented for the occasion, as with jazz. An important subcategory is songs sung during work, especially by nineteenth-century sailors at sea or by African women grinding grain, in which their performance is likely to be gendered, like the work itself. The rhythm of the song helps to coordinate heavy or repetitive labour, to distract from a tedious task or simply to celebrate joint activity.

The ballad is a form of narrative song that arose in Europe during the Middle Ages and hence is arguably part of a mixed oral–literary (or lecto-oral) tradition. The genre displays strong metrical forms associated with a melodic accompaniment; it is often concerned with warlike, noble conflict (especially in the Scottish-English border ballads of the fifteenth and sixteenth centuries), celebrating heroes and outlaws, but has held its popularity in the modern period, as exemplified in popular songs such as 'Frankie and Johnny' or Auden's 'Miss Gee'. Narrative songs of this kind are much less common in purely oral cultures, though varieties of the form mark some early literate societies; the Gilgamesh legend of Mesopotamia is an example.

Songs are distinguished from chant by being shorter and more melodic. Chant is a rhythmic manner of presenting speech that verges on recitation; while it may be accompanied, it is carried out with a regular beat that does not interfere greatly with the words, which are deemed more important than the music. Chant may be used for shorter recitals such as the Maori haka, a war chant that is accompanied by rhythmic movements, stamping of the feet and fierce gestures, and is sometimes employed for epic poetry or for the long recitations typically categorized as myth, as with the Bagre of the LoDagaa of northern Ghana.

Theatre in the modern sense is an outcome of the written tradition in Greece, Europe, India, Japan and elsewhere. However, it is sometimes difficult to draw a distinction between drama and ritual; indeed, the origins of both Greek and European drama lie in religious and ritual performances, as does Eastern puppet theatre that employs tales from Indian mythology. The occurrence of secular drama in oral cultures is not well attested and, where it does occur, is always peripheral as a cultural activity. There is often some reluctance to represent others at all, of which the use of masks as disguise is some indication; it is not a person but a category, another, that is being represented. Nevertheless (folk) plays of a more or less secular kind do occur in the popular (lecto-oral) culture of literate societies, such as the mumming plays of the European tradition, which stand in opposition to the written plays of the elite theatre.

Ritual has recently been analysed under the rubric of performance, a category that would include drama and represents an attempt to bring together the sacred and the secular in one analytical frame. While it is true that drama, as in the cases mentioned, may have its origin in sacred performances, to group them together is to ignore the intentions of the authors, which are very different in the two cases. The mass, for example, is a performance but one that involves worship addressed to a divinity, whereas theatre involves imaginative construction and a quite different kind of experience and audience. In Judaism and in Islam, as in early Christianity, ritual was performed but drama was proscribed. Only later did secular theatre re-emerge. The Abrahamistic religions forbad figurative representation, even at folk level where mummings were disapproved of. The tradition of classical theatre only returned to Europe with the Renaissance, with the diminishing importance of religious tenets. Secular theatre of course existed previously in classical times at Indian courts and among Japanese merchants, as the result of writing. Like the novel, much poetry (for example, the sonnet), the encyclopedia, the dictionary and the theatre are products of the written rather than the purely spoken word.

MYTH

Myth is a particular form of oral literature, the subject of which is partly cosmological. It was earlier thought that many such stories were explanatory. A few stories undoubtedly are, including those of the 'that is why the camel has a hump' variety (not a myth), but most are not, although intellectual curiosity (expressed through the notion of the quest) is often incorporated. For some commentators, myth was central to folktales: the meaning of folktales was seen to derive from their assumed status as broken-down myths, generated by linguistic misunderstandings and thought to account for solar, meteorological, or other natural phenomena. Other commentators (such as representatives of the myth and ritual school at the beginning of the twentieth century) have seen the explanation of myth as an accompaniment to ritual and of ritual as accompanying myth (as happens among the Navajo of North America). Such an explanation, however, does little to explain the content of myth or ritual. Others, such as Malinowski and the functionalist school, have understood myth as a legitimizing 'charter' of social institutions. Later in the twentieth century there was a move to interpretations in terms of a search for hidden meanings, some relying on psychoanalysis, others on different approaches to symbolic decoding, and yet others on structuralist analysis, especially in the work of Lévi-Strauss, which sought an underlying structure of abstract similarities (often binary in character) between a range of social institutions, to which the key often lay in myth.

Myth is often considered to be the highest achievement of oral literature. It has certainly proved to be the most attractive to outsiders and at the same time the most difficult to comprehend, because, even though it deals in cosmological matters, it is in some ways the most localized of genres, the most embedded in cultural action, sometimes being tied in a rather precise way to ritual activity (as when it is recited in a ceremonial context). Much of the oral literature of the Australian Aborigines, for example, has an essentially ceremonial function. The song cycles and narratives relate to the Dreaming, a mythological past in which the existing environment was shaped and humanized by ancestral beings. These performances may be open to the world at large (and hence be akin to entertainment) or closed to all but initiates.

It is important to distinguish here between contributions to mythologies, that is, accounts of worldviews constructed by observers, and myths in a narrower sense, which are actual recitations around a cosmological theme (for example, origin myths or creation stories). The latter are relatively rare and unevenly distributed around the world, being recited in particular, restricted circumstances, often on ritual occasions, as part, for example, of initiation rituals of secret societies. As such, the 'knowledge' they contain is not available to all but only to certain individuals, often of one sex. Among Australian Aborigines, for example, women are excluded from some ritual occasions. Yet these women, precluded from some knowledge, may also have parallel ceremonies from which men are excluded and during which women hand down different bodies of knowledge.

These myths were earlier thought to have been transmitted verbatim from one generation to the next, partly because that is how those who recited the myths often understood the situation. As such, they were interpreted as 'keys to culture', throwing a privileged light on society as a whole. But the advent of the portable audio recorder and of air travel enabled investigators to return at intervals to record such recitations in the actual context of performance, rather than with pencil and paper in a decontextualized situation. Several versions could be taken down. These new techniques showed that myths vary considerably over time, the exigencies of oral reproduction making such generative transmission a virtual necessity. People invent and fill in where they do not have perfect recall. One result is a plurality of versions spread over time (and space), but no fixed text such as we find with written literature, nor in the minds of earlier anthropologists who were only 'in the field' for a relatively short time.

LEGENDS AND HISTORICAL RECITATIONS

Legends and historical recitations – or 'histories' – occur everywhere: chiefless tribal societies produce stories of clan migration, for instance, while chiefly societies generate stories of the coming of rulers and of the establishment of kingdoms. Examples proliferate with writing and become more differentiated, but they exist in purely oral cultures as an important formal activity, to be told on ritual occasions, as with the Coming of the Kusiele in the Bagre ceremonies in northern Ghana or the many accounts of dynastic history found among the Asante of West Africa. These genres may also be associated with totemism, telling how a particular animal helped a past ancestor in troubled times and so its consumption or its killing became taboo to his or her descendants. The term legend (derived from the Latin *legenda*, 'to be read') was applied especially to the stories of saints in medieval Roman Catholic Europe and in contemporary Asia, but similar kinds of narrative, believed to be true, are also characteristic of oral cultures and later on often form the basis for the construction of written histories, as was the case in early Greece.

It is often forgotten that a purely oral society has a different approach to language than when writing intervenes. It is evanescent and cannot be studied, inspected, reviewed in the same way Eliot speaks of the 'interminable struggle with words and meanings'. This is usually an experience with writing but very rarely, if ever, with speaking. That is the difference between the two registers; speaking is extempore, writing involves 'thought', reflection, on what one writes, if only because it becomes a material object.

Even though a dead language is a concept relevant only in written cultures (in oral cultures language was never recorded, thus no one would know of them in the first place), some formalized historical recitations in purely oral cultures do retain earlier forms and content that have passed out of current usage. The speech of former generations can legitimize the material within a recitation, making that more valuable and more sacred at the time of the recitation, but it can also make the material less comprehensible, more mysterious, and more prone to conflicting and ambiguous interpretations. Such is the case with the 'drum histories', a set of chiefly titles beaten out on a drum and relating in a brief aphoristic way the story of the chiefdom, recited on state occasions by the Gonja of northern Ghana, where the tonal drum beats reflect the language. Their interpretation is difficult not only for strangers but for indigenes too. More broadly, histories are also often more concerned with legitimation, especially in providing a suggested link with the distant past, rather than intelligible in the story itself.

PERFORMANCE, CONTENT AND DISTRIBUTION

In oral cultures these various adult genres are not simply categories in a library catalogue but are part of an ensemble of actions that constitute the setting, often the ritual, and sometimes the music and dance of the performers; this includes a determination of the voice, gestures and the intentions of the performers, as well as of the audience and its expectations. Each genre has its characteristic context of performance, its own place, its own time, its own performers and its own aims. Myths, in the concrete sense, are likely to be recited not by ordinary people but by specialists in ritual contexts. Folktales may be told by adults who have built up a reputation for so doing, but they are more likely to make the rounds within families or among groups of children.

Given the variety of genres of oral literature, there is little one can say in general about their content. By definition mythology as a worldview deals with gods, deities and supernatural agencies in their relationship – whether distant or close – with humankind. Epics deal with human as well as with half-divine or even fully divine heroes and monsters. Folktales show a universal concern with animals, and they also introduce as actors humans, gods and sometimes monsters. The widespread inclusion of animals indicates a recognition of a continuity between living things; animals often re-enact the lives of humans, not only by actually speaking but in their roles (the chief of the animals) and in their actions (by holding moots). In this way they may also satirize human behaviour and point to lost possibilities, such as a misdirected message through which humanity missed the opportunity of immortality, conferred instead upon the snake or upon the moon. A continuity between living things is also expressed in tales of human beings born of animals, being cared for by them (as in the case of Romulus and Remus, the legendary founders of Rome), being looked after by them in a more mystical sense (as with the North American notion of the guardian spirit or in versions of totemism where humankind is aided by or even descended from a protected animal). The 'descent of man' is marked by this mixing of species, including humans and gods or animals and gods. One particular role that occurs in many tales is that of the trickster, often an animal such as the North American coyote or the spider in West Africa; trickster tales may also feature a fox or a hare. This trickster is a highly intelligent animal, acting in a human way but sometimes too clever for its own good. This use of animals, whether tricksters or not, is part of a widespread feature of oral genres, especially folktales, that admix all living things, humans and others, whereas in written cultures fiction takes on a more realistic character, humans speak to other humans. It also fits with the character of folktale as child-oriented. While similar genres are found widely distributed in oral cultures and in oral traditions, they do occur more centrally in some places than in others. For instance, in Western Europe, it is the Irish who are seen as most addicted to popular storytelling, whether about contemporary events or about traditional material. For much more specific reasons, the Roman Catholic countries of southern Europe continue to encourage the telling of saints' stories (or legends, a feature of the oral tradition of written cultures), whereas these stories almost entirely disappeared from the Protestant north when the saints themselves were largely banished.

Similarly, the long recitations defined above as myths are very unequally distributed even in neighbouring societies that otherwise display rather similar practices and beliefs, for they occur only under very restricted conditions. Epics and histories are associated with warrior and chiefly societies, respectively. Equally, there appears to be little use of proverbs and riddles among Native Americans, unlike in Africa, where collections of proverbs (such as those made in Asante by the Swiss missionary J. G. Christaller) were very common.

The content of myths and legends is considered to be true; by contrast, the content of folktales and fables is believed to be fictional. While the myths and legends are tied to particular societies (and later to particular written religions), the folktales and fables travel relatively freely between groups, including linguistic ones. That ability to travel reaffirms the fact that both have a different 'truth' status, with folktales rarely tied to specific cosmologies but instead showing a more universal appeal, especially to children. The common notion that adults regularly sit around a campfire and listen to tales of this kind seems to underestimate the levels of sophistication of those individuals. *Märchen* (folktales with an element of the magical or supernatural) and ghost stories have a wide appeal and are features of both oral and written literature told orally; tales of monsters are found in many societies, and even specific types, such as dragons, turn up over large areas. Fairies and trolls are found yet more frequently as characters in folktales and cosmologies, operating as intermediaries between humankind and the higher deities, the activities of which they both help and hinder. Earlier scholars sometimes saw these characters as recollections of some vanished pygmy people, whether in Africa or in Europe. There is no evidence of such a widespread distribution of these individuals, though we do find pygmy peoples in Africa, in Indonesia and elsewhere.

Once again, attempts to explain 'rationally' and 'historically' (but speculatively) the contents of oral literature have led the enquiry down false paths. As with oral literature in general it is essential to consider the context of performance and of transmission. Their imaginative and fictional character needs to be brought more prominently into the picture, including the interplay between man and gods. Not only with gods but with animals and all nature with which folktales often deal. We heard these tales as children and for children, often travelling from place to place, whereas myths and legends are more clearly tied to particular cultures or religions.

CHAPTER 3

The anthropologist and the audio recorder

Chapters 3 and 4 were published in France, the first in Régis Debray's journal, *Médium, transmettre pour innover*, in 2005, the second contribution was for a conference in Paris. In the first I discuss the role of the audio recorder for the anthropologist. This was critical to me personally and theoretically. Acquiring an early Philips machine in the field, after my original stay among the LoDagaa, meant that I could now record speech in recitation in a manner no one before had been able to do in 'primitive' situations. Not only could one now record in the actual context of performance, instead of having to take an 'informant' into one's hut, but also one had the opportunity to review the actual recitation at leisure. That was already something. For when one asked an 'informant' to recite, he was more likely to give you what you wanted to hear (the narrative bits, for example, leaving out the philosophical ones). But from my point of view what was most important was that, as distinct from working with pencil and paper in a field situation, one could now record with relative ease a plurality of versions of a single recitation. That was important because, in the case of the Bagre, these showed considerable variation, whereas if I believed the actors themselves, every version was the same (that is, in the same ritual). That showed me what Bartlett had demonstrated long ago,[1] that the unreliability of oral memory necessitated some reconstruction, quite apart from the wish to be creative. This understanding meant for me a revolution not only in the understanding of the role of 'myth' in oral societies but also in the whole appreciation of 'primitive mentality'. Myth could no longer be seen as tied to the rest of their social

---

[1] Bartlett 1932.

structure as Malinowski (for functional analysis) and Lévi-Strauss (for the structural variety) reasonably assumed, as they had only one version to work from; with considerable variations more allowance had to be made for independent change, for creation and for invention, for intellectual exploration, as in later forms of 'written literature' (though rarely varying in the same way). Secondly, this feature of society showed that in certain ways (not the technological and the scientific to be sure) they were less static and immobile than classical theories of 'traditional' society would suggest (and therefore less 'non-rational', 'non-logical' as well). As much had been suggested in Evans-Pritchard's well-known comments on Lévy-Bruhl but more specifically in Barth's study of change among neighbouring peoples of New Guinea.[2] Indeed, much cultural invention (in the narrower sense of the word) took place in Africa when one looks at the considerable variation in the rituals of neighbouring peoples in, for example, the Voltaic area, as distinct from the relative uniformity of agricultural production. Indeed, the following chapter on oral creativity deals with precisely this point.

My first visit to the LoDagaa, in the north-west of Ghana, dates from 1950. At the time it was difficult to record the melodies of their xylophone or even their recitations, long and elaborate as they were. To record sounds required heavy machines, which were both chunky and costly. To make them work needed electricity, which was only available when a village had its own generator. I myself had only pencils and paper. These were of no help in recording their music, as I was incapable of using musical notation. As for taking down their speech, that raised practical considerations which had their own problems in one way or another. Prayers were formal and were recomposed from memory or with the help of an assistant. In both cases, we were outside the context of the ceremony in which they were spoken.

Occasionally I persuaded an 'informer' to sit with me. He gave me an account of a procedure, a rite, an incident or even of his personal experiences. Then I wrote what he said directly in my notebook. But 'participant observation', so dear to anthropologists, only allowed one to scribble a note from time to time. You looked at them later on to reconstruct the day's happenings. It was difficult to

[2] Evans-Pritchard 1937; Barth 1987.

do any better, without taking time out. To film would have enabled one to reconstruct various scenes, but concentrating on one objective prevented one from seeing what went on around it. Hence the imperative, for those who worked after Malinowski, to write up one's fieldnotes that same evening, when the memory of the discussions was still fresh. It was always possible to ask the subjects to speak slowly, with many pauses, and to take full notes. I proceeded in this way when I took down the Bagre performance. I had been present at the public ceremonies of this initiation in the village of Birifu. An old soldier, Benima 'Dagarti', noticed me. He proposed to recite for me the 'myth' which was told to the initiates and to which I had no access. This recitation was given in the central room of the Bagre house where the public part of the ceremony took place. Benima himself was differentiated by the discovery of Islam (and especially its mosques) during his service overseas with the British army in southeast Asia. On his return, he left his local community and went to live in a nearby Muslim settlement. He continued to visit his natal village to keep up with his friends and to sell his medicines. In the eyes of both communities, he was regarded as a stranger, as the converted often were. But on becoming a Muslim, he was nevertheless still an initiate of the Bagre and had been instructed in the recitation by his grandfather. One day when he paid me a visit, he began the recitation. In order to make sense of what he told me I punctuated his dictation with questions. In the margins of my transcription, I added brief explanations of what he said by way of response. We continued this for ten days, in secret; he had broken his oath to the Bagre god.

Our meeting was critical. It permitted me to produce a 'text' of the myth of the Bagre. Aided by Romulo Tadoo, newly graduated from a Christian school, I embarked upon a translation a little later, in another village (Gwo and then Tom). This first meeting enabled me to overcome some of the limits of fieldwork, before the coming of the small, portable audio recorder, which captured the formal and informal speech in ritual ceremonies. It was very difficult to ask people to repeat funeral orations privately, for they felt very uncomfortable acting this way. As far as long 'mythical' recitations, like the Bagre, were concerned, repetitions were almost impossible – firstly, because of its secret character; but also because it was difficult to find a Speaker. Finally, the context of the ceremony itself was necessary in order to inspire someone, to give him voice. And even when these difficulties had been overcome, the recitation could never be the same as in the actual ceremony. It is not unreasonable to think that before the decade of the 1940s, most of what we look upon as oral literature was never in reality recited in this way during the ceremony itself. At best it was given in translation in completely decontextualized circumstances and by someone free from the constraints of public recitation. This is one reason why so often we have little data on the audience. At the moment of the recording, there was none – only the anthropologist him- or herself. So tales are often recorded with almost no information about their public and the conditions of delivery. What one thought was aimed at parents could be aimed at children (or anthropologists). In this way, one's enquiry only produced evidence of a mentality in a special sense, the equivalent of our nursery tales.

What are the other consequences of decontextualization? First of all, the Speaker will direct his attention to the audience present at that moment, and so anticipate what might be its interest. He often concentrated upon the narrative elements of the myth, excluding other sections that were less easy to recall, or less relevant to the situation. The result may be a distortion of the nature of myth. With the Bagre, I found important differences depending on the way it was recorded. The first version by Benima was markedly longer and more complicated than those recorded on the machine. Why? Benima was a serious and intelligent person. I will explain the differences in terms of the circumstances. Outside the ritual context itself, Benima was in a more relaxed position to develop certain themes in a rather free fashion, perhaps thinking that I would be more interested in the speculative and religious aspects. Dictation was also very difficult from the rapid recitations made to initiates. No pause to memorize is allowed; the good reciter is one who speaks quickly, fluently, clearly and without hesitation. On the contrary, Benima had to allow time to write down the myth and also to explain certain passages which seemed obscure to me. The whole process was much longer and more deliberate: ten days instead of eight hours, a period of time which allowed one to reflect on what one said.

The arrival of the audio recorder changed the picture. We could now record during the ceremony and translate afterwards. This new procedure had many advantages. Firstly, it enabled one to document what occurred during the ceremony. We could then understand the effect of the audience on the performance; for example, did they correct the Speaker? In the course of the Bagre, the audience members make only a few remarks, and not all the time. We could also analyse the way the recitation unfolds, because we recorded the mistakes, the gaps in memory as well as the continuities. But above all we could make several recordings of the same recitation and compare the similarities and the differences between the versions. In earlier times, anthropologists usually only wrote down one version. Unique, it became the point of reference. From that, one worked on the relations between a myth and a ritual, and even between a myth and the society in which it arose, while neglecting the possible existence of variations of that myth. This single version was seen as the standard and normalized form, transmitted from generation to generation in a relatively precise manner.

One single allusion to the machine was made in our first recording. It was incorporated into the version recited, a definite indication of change. Sometime later in Gonja, where I was present on the occasion of the birth of the Prophet, I had carefully brought my recorder. In order to record the prayers of the Muslims, I placed it in front of me, as discreetly as possible. After several minutes, a rich trader, Abu Jaja, got up to fetch his own recorder, then took mine and placed the two in the centre of the scene, right in front of the Speakers. The machine had made its entry into that culture, even if it eroded the monopoly on the oral transmission of knowledge and its secrets.

Our recordings showed considerable variations, whether they were made by the same person in different situations or by different persons in the same situation, proof that the Bagre is not remembered by heart, word for word, a hypothesis which I adopted at the beginning. In actual practice, the Speakers recall certain passages, more or less. They memorize a series of themes and a method of recitation. The variations are not secretly introduced but are encouraged (it remains 'one'), even if they mean the disappearance of another theme. These versions show the presence of creative talents which the idea of a fixed text of a myth overlooks. Finally, one must note that this process of creation is also going on in the neighbouring villages.

The introduction of the audio recorder in work in the social sciences reveals a flexible relation between myth and society. This looseness must be acknowledged in contrast to the supposition of many earlier anthropologists. The recitation of a myth is not simply an exercise in exact reproduction, as if one was copying a passage of Milton's *Paradise Lost*. On the contrary, it involves the incremental creation of a large number of variants, which results not simply in changes in the surface structure but also in the deep structure of myth. Certainly, there always exists a level of abstraction which can reduce the different versions to variants of a Proppian kind. But in the case of the Bagre, the variations affect the whole tone of the recitation. Important elements which I had thought permanent (the visit to God) disappeared in later versions, almost without leaving a trace. So it was impossible to predict what constituted the deep continuing structure of the myth. And one was struck by differences similar to those in the discourse of written culture.

These new techniques have allowed us to review our theoretical conclusions; paper and pencil are no longer the only instruments at our disposal. The recorder is a long way from solving all our analytic problems. It forms one of our tools, in the fashion of the computer. As I have said, the publication of a fixed transcription in a 'text' replaces the creative heterogeneity of the myth with an authoritarian orthodoxy. The recording of different versions does more than reveal to us that there are serious problems about the hypothesis of an original source. It also shows creativity and the existence of versions which propose different ways of understanding the world, which may also be contradictory of one another.

CHAPTER 4

Oral creativity

Societies without writing are often considered to be static, traditional, handing down their culture from generation to generation. That idea has been encouraged by many anthropologists who have seen the 'ethnographic present' as describing a culture fixed by unchanging custom. It is an idea often supported by the 'natives' themselves. 'The world is always as it was', the German anthropologist Franz Boas was told by the Eskimos, as if to deny the very notion of history. History, the scholar of literature Ian Watt and I argued, began with the written word. It was the printers, Franklin declared, who put us in perpetual motion. And we moderns are accustomed to a world that is ever-changing.

However, the traditional world according to Weber is static, unchanging to Braudel. Wallerstein sees the incessant search for change, for profit, as being the defining feature of capitalism (a notion derived from Rostow).[1] Whereas traditional societies are governed by custom, not by rationality, and each generation accepts unquestioningly what its predecessor had laid down. How far is this true of earlier societies? There are certain segments where change, especially material change, is slow, in agriculture for example. That is why the societies remain 'primitive'. But even here, change takes place over time, in the shape of a hand axe, in the creation of auxiliary tools. But there are other areas of social life where change is much more in evidence.

For example, in the sphere of ritual and religion there is considerable variation even between neighbouring peoples. That is quite understandable. In the first place, the exact repetition of long

---

[1] Wallerstein 1999.

rituals, despite all intentions, is difficult to preserve over time, especially if they are performed only at long intervals. Variations creep in partly because memory is imperfect and people do the best they can. That process is even clearer with the words that accompany ritual, especially those long recitations that we speak of as 'myths'. Anthropologists who have recorded these recitations with pencil and paper, a laborious and difficult task in itself, have often thought that they were recording a fixed version, because the people themselves had spoken of all versions as being 'the same'. Consequently we have considerable discussions about the role of memory in oral cultures, as compared with the apparently failing memories of literate societies where people can depend for recall upon what has been written down in a book. It is possible that some societies have developed a system of oral mnemonics for certain limited purposes. One thinks of the use of material objects such as stools in Asante for memorizing royal genealogies and deeds, and of similar processes in the Pacific. It has been reported that the Rig Veda is passed down orally by Brahmans in India. But this is a literate society, there are written versions to refer to, and one of the main mnemonic techniques, the system of rhyme, seems largely to depend on writing, or the visual interiorization of the word. But firstly oral mnemonics are unusual and secondly until the advent of the audio recorder we had no real means of establishing identity over time.

My own work on versions of the Bagre recitation of the LoDagaa of northern Ghana, collected over a period of some twenty years with the help of Kim Gandah,[2] which in discussion the reciters declare to be 'one' (the same), shows considerable variations, not simply of a superficial kind but in the very structure of the myth and its basic themes (these I have discussed in much greater detail in Chapter 6).

There seems little doubt that in the Black Bagre, which is the more imaginative of the two parts of the main recital, the Speakers are concerned about the relation of mankind with the world in which they find themselves, especially about the supernatural elements within it, some repeating (as best they can), some elaborating, some speculating. These speculations vary within a range of possibilities, much as accounts of the European universe varied among the less orthodox

[2] Goody 1972; Goody and Gandah 1981, 2000.

Christians who were investigated by the Inquisition[3] and who were not held back by orthodox beliefs. Imagination or 'fancy' is not the prerogative of one culture or type of cultures. And there is forgetting as well as creation; indeed, in oral cultures they are two sides of the same coin. Forgetting requires invention, creation; creation probably requires some forgetting. That applies even to the first part, which is less speculative in that it provides a commentary – a guide and perhaps something of an explanation – on the long series of rituals themselves, during the course of which the White Bagre is repeatedly recited. Some Speakers make mistakes in the order of the ceremonies; all are obviously incomplete as accounts, some more so than others. Even where Speakers recite in the same performance or where the same speaker recites again soon after an earlier performance, the versions differ, more as one would expect with different Speakers than with the same, since each one internalizes, in a more or less exact manner, his own version, and produces it on request. Nevertheless, even here there are variations since it is almost impossible, under oral conditions, where there is no text of reference, to learn a long recitation 'by heart'. There is forgetting, and there is creation, if only to fill the gaps. That applies not only to the order of the ceremonies but to the aspects of their content selected for presentation. All in all, there is no way that this aspect of the oral 'myth' can be considered as static, and that presents us with a very different picture of the place of 'myth' in those cultures, not fixed and unitary, but diversifying and multiple, as well as of the place of creativity in them.

It was not only verbally that there was invention, although one reason that the White Bagre was less variable than the Black was certainly that the White was more closely tied to the series of ceremonies, the sequence and contents of which could be more readily recalled. Nevertheless, there was creation in the sphere of ritual, that is, standardized actions oriented to the supernatural. How else can we explain the variations in, say, formal ceremonies concerning birth or death among the particular groups in northern Ghana? There were certainly some external points of reference, Islam, for example. But much of the variation does seem to be of internal origin. Let us take the events that accompanied the funeral of 'Chief' Gandah of Birifu

[3] Ginsberg 1980; Le Roy Ladurie 1978.

in 1949. At one point in the course of the final funeral ceremony (*ko dāā gbaaro*), I was surprised to witness the arrival of an open lorry, the occupants of which consisted of an entire brass band, loudly playing their instruments. The band had driven up several hundred miles from a village near Kumasi in Asante from whence many years before a delegation had come to acquire the shrine of *kungpenbie* from the late Chief, who had himself got it from the nearby Dagaba, a related but somewhat different ethnic group. In Asante the shrine had done very well, that is to say, that as trade and commerce were expanding, a number of clients who had come to consult it had prospered and had shared their prosperity with the owners of the shrine which they considered partly responsible for their success. The Asante owners had in turn shared some of this wealth with the Chief of Birifu, even providing him with a truck with which his son, Kumbɔɔno, later traded between Kumasi and the north.[4] The dispatch of the band and its noisy arrival at the funeral constituted part of the more or less final phase of the transfer of the shrine, but one which was likely to influence LoDagaa funerals in the future. It was customary to celebrate, at a large funeral, all the various sources from which an individual had profited during his life, acting as a ferryman, playing the xylophone, owning a successful shrine. If they were new ways of doing things and new ways of celebrating these (as with the band), these were likely to be repeated in the future, such as the playing of different forms of music in addition to the 'traditional' xylophone and drums.

Clearly these new modifications in the funeral service reflect wider changes in the economy. But the possibility of change is not new. In the ritual sphere that has been so over the long term, as with linguistic dialects; otherwise it would be impossible to account for the local variation emerging over a fairly limited space and indeed time. One sees the same process taking place with certain types of shrine. Once again one cannot account for the emergence of shrines such as *kungpenbie* and Tigari without presuming a process of continuous creation and obsolescence. 'Medicine shrines' of this kind have been a constant feature of African societies in the post-colonial period, often specializing in protection against witchcraft but also in

---

[4] See Gandah 2004.

other aspects associated with the new economy, increased commerce and the role of motor vehicles, for example. Some authors have tied their appearance to the new conditions of uncertainty under which contemporary Africans are living, and certainly this situation is likely to produce more shrines and to increase the circulation of existing ones. But to see 'medicine shrines' as an entirely new category in this situation seems to me wrong and to reflect a mistaken view of unchanging earlier cultures. There are historic reports of the movement of such shrines from one place to another and that is quite understandable. Any shrine that purports to offer a cure for human woes is bound to come under pressure when, for instance, the witches it has purported to chase away make their return, or when the recurrent possibility of an epidemic such as sleeping sickness returns to the area. In these cases, a person may search around for a new way of dealing with the problem, whether brought in from outside or possibly created in the area.

I had a friend, called Betchara, who worked very much on his own, partly as a ferryman. One day he offered to take me to see his new shrine on the banks of the Black Volta River. Physically it consisted of a stick, some 50 cm in height, round which had been fastened bundles of grass. He told me that he had constructed his *tïïb* at the behest of the beings of the wild, who are especially preoccupied with water and any monies derived from crossing rivers. The beings of the wild (*kontome*) are often called fairies or dwarfs in English, resembling as they do those creatures in European folklore. But they are more serious and more central to LoDagaa religion, their anthropomorphic shrines being connected with divination and with the revelation to humankind of the secrets of the other world and the problem of sacrifice to its agencies. In the course of such revelation, the beings may point to a creative cause, such as the need to establish a new shrine as well as to make an offering to an old one. Indeed, they are attributed with the power to instruct humankind in the ways of God (*Na'ŋmin*), which is the Creator God, and in one account has given humans, through the beings of the wild, the main features of their cultural repertoire. Some versions of the Bagre are connected in a major way with the transmission of culture to humanity, the brewing of beer and the making of iron, paradigmatically, in the creation of those processes that are at the core of humans' existence upon earth.

So, even with regard to technology and similar matters, the world is not always as it was, as the Eskimo reputedly claimed according to Boas, but there has been a creative process at work, in some versions of which the role of humans themselves is more creative than in others.

However, looked at from the outside, those spheres of technology are slower to change than that of religion and possibly 'culture' in a non-material sense. Looking around the different societies of northern Ghana, their agricultural technology is much the same, and comparatively static, even over the longer *durée*. It did change with the introduction of new American crops by the Portuguese, and of South Asian ones by others. But here there is little enough room for invention. That is not at all the case in religious matters. Although there are some similarities at the level of the major supernatural agencies, especially the High God, the Earth as well as the Rain, the ancestors, even the beings of the wild, at other levels there is great variation. Some groups use masks, to others they are anathema, an unnecessary disguise. Such differences are emergent. So too are many shrines, some attached to particular localities with particular meanings, which often change with the passage of time. Even kinship, so often seen as part of the core structure, varies considerably between adjacent groups in ways that seem to have been generated by difficulties with a pre-existing system, such as complications in the inheritance of a person's wives. Shifts on a larger scale between matrilineal and patrilineal reckoning take place, as I have hypothesized among subgroups of the LoDagaa themselves. Undoubtedly there is a tendency for such arrangements to repeat themselves over adjacent generations – that is what cultural transmission is about, but the fixity of these arrangements has often been much exaggerated in the imposition on the simpler societies of an almost biological view of culture. You've got what you came with at birth!

CHAPTER 5

The folktale and cultural history

In a well-known book, Darnton (1984) has taken the folktale as an example of 'primitive thought'. I argue that the audience for these tales is not normally adult, but it is as if other societies were taking 'Jack and the Beanstalk' as a representation of contemporary Britain. Folktales are often international and do not reflect any particular social system, except in a very peripheral way, as they are freely communicated.

In the first chapter on folktales of his book on French cultural history in the eighteenth century, Robert Darnton attempts to get at the mentalities, the consciousness, of a peasant population which is also seen as representative of a wider constituency, namely France itself. He compares and contrasts English and German folktales with a view to determining their Frenchness.[1] This enterprise he distinguishes from 'romantic rhapsodizing about national spirit' or the notion of a *Volksgeist*,[2] but an element of this type of generalization is nevertheless present. For example, he sees the folk stories as having a common style and exhibiting the theme of trickery that is considered to be an enduring feature of French culture. That characterization is often made of the French peasant but it could reasonably be claimed to be equally true of many other cultures, as Scott has argued.[3] And in any case, as countless folklorists have observed, the similarities in tales across cultures are as significant as the differences. And the generalized differences at this level are very difficult to assess, even by as sensitive a writer as Darnton undoubtedly is.

It is the use of folktales on which I want to remark, partly for their own sake, partly as a comment on one form of 'cultural history'.

---

[1] This aspect of his study has been received critically by Chartier (1985).
[2] Darnton 1984: 61. [3] Scott 1976, 1985.

There are other forms of this; Jardine and Brotton proclaim a 'new cultural history' in their book *Global Interests*,[4] though the term came into historians' usage in the 1980s, and I myself would see included in cultural history the discussion of the significance of changes in the mode of communication (in particular, literacy). But before I turn to examining these questions, I want briefly to outline the scope of the rest of Darnton's study. In the second chapter, on the printer's attack on the cats, Darnton is concerned with the 'mentalité' of a work group – and how it constitutes part of the wider sociocultural scene. In the third he tackles the consciousness of an individual merchant in examining a municipal procession in Montpellier, which he considers as part of 'a basic element in eighteenth-century world views'.[5] And he sees his task not as discovering what the town looked like at that time but as how 'our observer observed it'. However, surely both are involved together in a comprehensive account, as Darnton certainly appreciates when he turns to discuss a 'description of the town' as it has been reconstructed by historians.[6]

Darnton's interest in the *procession générale* of Montpellier was not as a replication of the social structure but as expressing 'the essence of society',[7] a complex aim that defies definition. Other chapters deal with a police file, the categories of knowledge and a reading of Rousseau, with a conclusion tackling some general points in cultural history. But it is the first chapter and the use of folktales that concerns me here.

Darnton uses 'tales' (folktales, 'fairy tales') to illuminate 'the mental world [the essence?] of the unenlightened during the Enlightenment',[8] looking for the world, the mentality, of the common man in an attempt to reconstruct French cultural history. As an anthropologist interested in history, just as Darnton is a historian interested in anthropology, I want to comment upon this enterprise, a comment that will involve a discussion of the role of the folk in folklore.

While anthropological analysis can help historical research by introducing a comparative as well as a more systematic spatial dimension (just as history can help anthropology deal with change and the

---

[4] Jardine and Brotton 2000.   [5] Darnton 1984: 109.   [6] Darnton 1984: 114.
[7] Darnton 1984: 114.   [8] Darnton 1984: 9.

time dimension), system building also has its negative aspect if it ceases to be sensitive to the material. And that is just the problem of the holistic approach, whether structural or functional. While these approaches rightly call upon the enquirer to look for interrelationships between, say, politics and family, they may well overstress the overall unity of 'cultures'. For instance, it would never be possible to discuss dress in contemporary Africa in those terms, as the uniform of schoolchildren as of nurses has reference to social interaction quite outside any specific culture; even if this has a local meaning ('local knowledge'), the wider significance has to be taken into account.

One of the problems that 'cultural history' faces, which 'social history' does not, is that it tends to treat culture, in the manner of certain anthropologists, as an undifferentiated whole. That was the sense of Tylor's definition of 'culture' in 1871 and Darnton draws the comparison with Thoms' use of 'folklore' in 1846. The folk and its lore are seen as an unstratified, unlocalized, sometimes atemporal unity, at least at the level of the common man, or the 'unenlightened' in Darnton's phrase. Culture too makes similar holistic assumptions which have been central to much of the American tradition of anthropology, for example, in the work of Geertz, with whom Darnton conducted a continuing seminar at Princeton. That tradition differs from the earlier British one which aimed at analysing social structure rather than culture. It differs too from a vaguely Marxist treatment of stratification in the history of culture, for example, in the writings of E. P. Thompson and Raymond Williams.

I do not see much profit in discussing social life at this level of abstraction, especially as such positions tend to slant the analysis in their own direction. The social structural approach tends to dwell on the 'surface structure'; the culture as an epiphenomenon of an underlying structure. That view tends to give too little emphasis to the actor's frame of reference and has in turn holistic tendencies, especially in the work of Lévi-Strauss and the French structuralists (who in the realm of folklore hark back to Propp). What a study of social organization and social history should do for 'culture', in the sense of performance, is to draw attention to its stratified nature, stratified not only in the sense of class but in terms of age and gender. To take age, extracts from the *Boy's Own Paper* or from the likes of Henty's adventure stories do not throw much light on the mentality of adults or of girls, even though phylogenetically, developmentally, they may in some cases have contributed to their final make-up. But I insist that in our culture no adult would willingly sit round a room and listen to 'Little Red Riding Hood', the tale Darnton chooses from which to elicit adult mentalities, and it seems quite wrong to think that the folk or more specifically our eighteenth-century ancestors would have done so either. Nor even in 'other cultures'. That assumption would be to demean their modes of thought and to perpetuate the notion of a wide and unexplained gap, the Great Divide, between them (the other, the 'unenlightened', the folk) and us. Reason argues otherwise. So too do my contemporary experiences in Africa. And I would need very substantial evidence from our own past to convince me otherwise.

The Great Divide is a gap to which Darnton (like others) thinks I subscribe. But my attempt in the writings to which he referred was to try and elucidate the background of the assumptions that others have made. I did so by insisting upon the specific (but not the exclusive) role of changes in the means of communication, which were multiple not binary (and include the woodblock, the press, the typewriter and the computer), in order to set aside unexplained binary categorizations of others such as enlightened and unenlightened, modern and traditional, advanced and primitive. I may be pointing to the wrong mechanism but at least I am doing so from a concrete sociohistorical perspective, which needs to be refuted or supplemented at the same level of analysis. Darnton is quite right, of course, to insist that 'tale telling can flourish long after the onset of literacy',[9] but the whole genre is strongly influenced by its advent and particularly by the coming of 'print culture'! The division of oral from written cultures to which he refers is not the same as that between the use of the oral and written registers, which is what he is really talking about. This marks what I call lecto-oralty, oral transmission in a society with writing.

Such tales as Darnton deals with, 'Red Riding Hood' above all, were known as nursery tales in England since at least the time of Richardson's *Pamela*.[10] So if he is right 'that peasant raconteurs in late nineteenth century France tell stories to one another pretty

---

[9] Darnton 1984: 28.   [10] Richardson 1741.

much as their ancestors had done a century or more earlier', at both historical periods we would have to accept that 'fairy tales' were largely 'nursery tales' and aimed at children rather than at adults, as the name implies. Even in Darnton's own account some of the tales are recognized as directed to children,[11] and often 'tend to be cautionary'.[12]

In English the concept of 'fairy tales' occurs at roughly the same time as 'nursery tale', being a translation of the French, *conte de fées*. Its first appearance was in 1749 in the letters of Horace Walpole. And not long after it took on the other meaning of falsehood, in the same way as tale in the phrase 'telling tales'. Darnton prefers the term 'folktale' to these actor concepts since it enables him to refer to peasant culture in general rather than only to 'childish things'. But that does not seem to have been a category of the folk themselves and indeed should perhaps be seen as covering a plurality of genres, indigenous or indeed analytic.

The notion of a tale used by Darnton in the title of his chapter covers of course not only fairy tales but other forms of *contes* including accounts of the happenings at last week's village market. So too does the word folktale in the usage, for example, of the contemporary scholar of folklore, Alan Dundes. My argument depends heavily on deconstructing this nineteenth-century blanket term and distinguishing between different forms of narrative.

Notions of truth and historicity as distinct from fiction (telling tales) and indeed myth (though there the criteria are observer rather than actor generated) are constantly raised in the analysis of folklore, though this may seem an old-fashioned concern to many. Lowie, who wrote the ethnology of the Crow Indians, found that their 'oral traditions' were without 'historical value'.[13] Darnton takes this as meaning 'factual accuracy', but Lowie was perhaps reaching further. Dundes notes that most hero narratives are, or were, told as true stories; they are legends rather than fairy tales.[14] All are included in folklore, a term which Dundes sees as covering not only the activities of unlettered persons in societies with writing (in nineteenth-century fashion) but as including the thoughts and actions of 'primitive'

---

[11] Darnton 1984: 62.   [12] Darnton 1984: 53.   [13] Lowie 1935.
[14] Dundes 1980: 131.

peoples (presumably in societies without writing) on the one hand and urban populations (folk in societies dominated by literacy) on the other; in other words what E. B. Tylor called culture. In his conclusion to his discussion of folktales, Darnton refers to the two cultures of storytelling. People like Perrault heard these from 'wet nurses and nannies, who lulled them to sleep with popular songs and amused them, after they had learned to talk, with *histoires ou contes du temps passé* ... that is, old wives' tales. While the *veillée* perpetuated popular traditions within the village, servants and wet nurses provided the link between the culture of the people and the culture of the élite.'[15] He goes on to explain how the Perrault versions and others were printed in the chapbooks of the *Bibliotèque bleue* which 'were read aloud at *veillées* in villages where someone was capable of reading'. The peasants and salon sophisticates 'did not inhabit completely separate mental worlds. They had a great deal in common – first and foremost, a common stock of tales' which 'communicated traits, values, attitudes, and a way of construing the world that was peculiarly French'.[16] But on his own reckoning they were for children among the elite and for adults among the illiterate. That is a Great Divide I find difficult to accept at the level of mentalities and which seems to demean peasant culture. One should be particularly careful about this way of looking at peasant societies when, despite the late age of marriage in Europe, boys turn into men and girls into women so quickly. In the French village where I wrote this essay boys of 12 and 14 were roaring around in tractors, much earlier on Mobylettes. In many ways they have put away childish things and are engaged in 'adult' productive tasks.

Understandably there were occasions in rural society when villagers sat around, such as the *veillées* in the French countryside. I myself have heard of such gatherings around the *cantou* in the Lot where even in the post-war period people came together to shell walnuts or dehusk maize, lengthy tasks that were best performed in common. Such gatherings have now disappeared, because, say those who attended, of the coming of the television, and the associated activities themselves have certainly seen a downturn. In the summer of 2001 I approached some friends in the south-west of France to speak to

---

[15] Darnton 1984: 63.   [16] Darnton 1984: 63.

older inhabitants and enquire what forms of discourse were undertaken in the course of the *veillées* and to what audience. Such an exercise always has its dangers since people are very prone to romanticize their past and to compare adulthood with childhood. Nevertheless, it seemed to be agreed that the content took the form of exchanging news (or 'gossip') on an informal basis. I see no evidence that adults would sit around telling each other 'nursery tales' (the equivalent of Perrault or Grimm) in the early twentieth century and find no reason why things should have been different in earlier times.

Folklorists dealing primarily with peasant cultures, that is, with the 'unenlightened', 'illiterate' segments of complex societies with writing, have tended to see their subjects as the backward, non-progressive, 'traditional' elements.[17] Hence they have often understood their task as tracing such activities back to earlier, 'primitive', forms much as Frazer did in his monumental work *The Golden Bough*. Of course, there are many forms of social thought and action that carry with them evidence of their cultural history. But it would be a great mistake not to recognize that all such acts are repositioned in the new context. That is to say, folk remedies have to be analysed both from the societal and individual standpoints in their relationship with (and interaction between) the learned tradition developed *inter alia* by Galen and Hippocrates, and practised by 'medical' specialists. The same is true of other aspects of belief systems. The shape of analogous beliefs in ancestral figures in peasant cultures is obviously totally different when the commanding heights of the religious life are occupied by a written world religion. That situation is precisely what we found in the former Yugoslavia, which was the locus of the comparison between Homeric bards and Balkan *guslari*. The presence of a written religion clearly affects the nature of the content of the relevant 'epics'; the latter obviously exclude any extensive treatment of major religious matters which are the domain of priests, of temples and of the Book, whether the Bible or the Quran. The existence of parallel written literature may influence such 'oral' forms in many ways.

It seems to me Darnton makes much of a Great Divide between the enlightened and the unenlightened, and at the same time suggests that I perpetuate a similar notion regarding literate and non-literate.

---

[17] Dundes 1980: chapter 1.

I'm not sure that I have ever divided the world into oral and written or print cultures, since in all cultures people communicate orally. But I do see difference between societies with and without writing, including differences in their oral forms (the narrative and the novel, for example), and it is difficult to understand how any history of human culture is possible without taking cognizance of such changes in the modes of communication. I regard this as a more enlightened way of explaining difference (even partially) than one based on enlightenment or even on the vague concept of mentality.

Darnton refers to the work of Parry and Lord on 'how folk epics as long as *The Iliad* are passed on faithfully from bard to bard among the illiterate peasants of Yugoslavia'.[18] He recognizes that they do not possess the 'fabulous powers of memorization sometimes attributed to "primitive" people'. Indeed, they 'do not memorise very much at all'. Each performance is unique. Nevertheless, 'recordings made in 1950 do not differ in essentials from those made in 1934'. Even printed material can be worked in, for 'modifications of detail barely disturb the general configuration'.[19] But what is this 'general configuration' and how would one configure it? Only, I suggest, by taking a series of versions (1934–50) and designating a common core. Common elements certainly exist over this period, but it is a rather short one. In addition, the printed sources of many of these epics undoubtedly constrain narration, since these are often being referred to. Some of the *guslari* were illiterate (but in what script?) but not all and those that could not read could still be strongly influenced by the printed sources, if only indirectly. Hence, as we have seen, one would expect much less variation there than in the case of a purely oral culture where there were no such mnemonics, no such constraints, no fixed text lying in the background. In any case, the epics are constantly being adapted to new situations as well as new ones being created. In the recent conflicts in the former Yugoslavia, bards on every side sometimes performed in the van of the fighting men, rather like Scottish pipers; their performance stirred up civilian morale and at least one prominent politician was also a major *guslari*. There was little static about this tradition.[20]

---

[18] Darnton 1984: 19.   [19] Darnton 1984: 19.

[20] I am indebted for information to Bojun Baskar as well as to contributors to the Mediterranean Summer School in Slovenia. He also provided me with a copy of a Croatian study of modern bards (Žanic 1998).

Darnton argues that Lord's work confirmed in Yugoslavia that of Propp's on Russian folktales, 'how variation of detail remains subordinate to stable structures'.[21] But Propp's stable structures are often so abstract that variation is scarcely conceivable since the alternative possibilities are so many. In any case, the genres are very different, epic and folktale, including performance, audience and structure. We rarely find long epics (or other long recitations) in purely oral cultures. Where we do, there is little to suggest great continuity over time – indeed, with the Bagre of the LoDagaa of northern Ghana,[22] as we will see, the variations are enormous. But folktales are different; there does seem to be some continuity over time, partly because such short tales can be more easily memorized, partly because stories we hear in early infancy may be more easily retained, as with language itself. Darnton also argues that in traditional societies 'continuities of form and style outweigh variations in detail'.[23] At this level of abstraction the same could be said of any culture, though one might well ask why should form 'outweigh' content?

There is a danger in assuming that in purely oral cultures, long recitations are memorized with great accuracy. In many cases they are not, and cannot be. When we come to the oral traditions in cultures with writing, the situation is different. If there is a version that has been printed, as with Perrault, then it may be read out or referred to, as Darnton suggests happened at *veillées*, when it provides a fixed text for the reciter to refresh his memory. Even so, there may be problems with writers assuming that oral forms operate in the same way as fixed texts. Darnton is critical of psychoanalytic attempts to interpret folktales, especially of Fromm's interpretation of 'Little Red Riding Hood', which he sees as attempting to decode the symbolic languages of the collective unconscious in primitive society. He comments that Fromm's version of the text was 'based on details that did not exist in the versions known to peasants in the seventeenth and eighteenth centuries'.[24] Psychoanalysis takes us into 'a mental universe that never existed', that did not appear 'in the original folktale'. But I wonder if one can talk about an original folktale. That idea goes back to the origin of oral forms, of which we can surely

[21] Darnton 1984: 19.   [22] Goody 1972; Goody and Gandah 1981, 2002.
[23] Darnton 1984: 20.   [24] Darnton 1984: 11.

have no knowledge, unlike that of a written text with its deliberately constructed stemma.

Let me return to the problem of the audience for oral genres which was raised earlier. The difficulty is that we do not have much satisfactory information on the context for the telling of tales, for example. The folktale specialist Stith Thompson continually talks of campfires. But when he discusses, following Botte, the use of folktales in Greece and Rome he writes: 'They told of fairies and monsters ... A frequent term used for them is "old women's stories", and authors keep referring to the telling of these tales to children'.[25] In his summary of the main points raised by scholars of folklore, there is no mention of the audience. In a sense, that is understandable because collectors needed to find individuals who would relate them the stories *out of context* so that they could write them down – recording in context would have been virtually impossible before the advent of the portable audio recorder.

But while observations on actual recitation before an audience were few, if not non-existent, many assumptions were made, some based on nostalgic constructions of life in the old days, gathered round a fire in the evening light. Some more definite assumptions were implied for example by the Grimms in the title of their collection *Kinder- und Hausmärchen*.[26] There was no doubt in their minds that at the beginning of the nineteenth century, children formed a central element of the audience.

One of the major problems in using this material, in determining the audience and the context of performance, is that of the vagueness of some definitions of genres. Stith Thompson's definition of the folktale is very wide. He sees narrative as universal, the form taken by reports of recent happenings, by legends or by fiction. In the west he claims narrative was cultivated in all ranks, extending from Homer to tales of medieval priests to 'the old peasant', who 'now as always, whiles away the winter evenings with tales of Goldilocks ... Poets write epics and novelists novels'.[27] However, he then goes on to say he is only dealing in 'the traditional prose tale' handed down; either in writing or by word of mouth, it is the essence that it is 'handed down'. The term 'folktale' for him includes these literary narratives,

---

[25] Thompson 1951: 272.   [26] Grimms 1819 (2nd edn).   [27] Thompson 1951: 3–4.

so that we are dealing not only with oral literature or that of unlettered 'folk'. These are said to resemble each other in their disregard of originality of plot or of pride of ownership; that is, the traditional tale, the folktale, which is in some sense 'oral'.[28] Traditional (as in storytelling) is a category that includes both oral cultures (as in the case of the Crow Indians) and written ones (as in the case of the Yugoslavian peasantry).

The category includes *Märchen* (folktales), novellas, hero tales, *Sagen* (legends), explanatory tales, myths, animal tales, fables, jests. The problem here is that the category becomes so wide that there is little one can say about it as a whole. For some elements are clearly aimed at adults, while others (I would contend) are for children: some are 'imaginary', others factual. For instance, when the American folklorist R. M. Dorson went to Ireland to witness the collection of folktales (or folklore), what he heard, in the company of the full-time collector Tradling Murphy, was stories, apparently believed to be true, about near contemporary events in the neighbourhood.[29] There is no problem about seeing such tales as directed to adults. But with others there is a question. Yet if you see all such tales as 'popular', as 'traditional', as coming from the folk, there certainly must be questions about the audience for some, at least, as to whether peasants really sat around listening to 'Goldilocks'.

At the conclusion of his valuable account of the folktale,[30] Stith Thompson writes of the decline of the oral tale, which has been overtaken by the cinema, as in the case of 'Snow White'.

Children of course, were very fond of it, for in our civilisation it is primarily the young child who carries on the interest in the folktale. In spite of the efforts of certain educators, these tales continue to be told in the nursery and later to be read in easy re-tellings. In fact, this situation is so well recognised that publishers and libraries are likely to class all folktales as juvenile literature. As a practical measure this attitude is justified, for adults in a world of books have given up these old stories as childish things. And yet we have seen that once everywhere these tales were not considered childish. They have been one of the chief forms of entertainment for all members of society, young and old. Even today in remote corners of our western world, and everywhere among primitive men, folktales serve to give artistic expression to the imagination and to bring amusement and excitement to

---

[28] Thompson 1951: 5.   [29] Dorson 1976.   [30] Thompson 1951.

monotonous lives. They will long continue to be one of the chief means of furnishing education and solace to unlettered men and women.[31]

The first assertions about the present are undoubtedly correct, but for the past they seem much more problematic. When is this adoption of the folktale by children supposed to have taken place? Thompson refers to the world of books having had this effect (presumably the printed book), to the cinema and elsewhere to the Enlightenment. The assumption is always about its earlier adult status.

That, of course, was true of the Grimms, for whom the origin of folktales lay in 'myths'. 'The mythic element, the significance of which has long been lost, expands the farther we go back'; 'indeed it seems to have formed the only subject of the oldest fictions'. The tales were 'broken down myths', which derived from Indo-European sources, epitomized in the Rig Veda. This they saw as 'the treasure house of mythology'.[32] In his introduction to his *Essai sur les fables indiennes*,[33] Deslongchamps saw all such tales as originating in India and diffused by Buddhism and Islam (to Europe). 'The transformations which tales experience … are … almost entirely a kaleidoscopic confusion of forms, traits, and motifs that were originally separated.'[34] But of course, as the Grimms seem to realize, these ancient narratives were not regarded as fiction by the people who heard them, so that folktales, which are self-evidentially fictional narratives, seem unlikely to have been their descendants. However, it is the case that elements of such tales may be included in myths and epics, as we find in Homer as well as in the Bagre, the long recitation of the LoDagaa of northern Ghana, which I have recorded, transcribed and published on several occasions.[35]

Darnton's use of folktales is linked to his wider concerns with 'cultural history'. A key moment in the proclamation of his endeavour comes in his criticism of the *Annales* school, which he recognizes as being the most important trend in history writing in the twentieth century, for trying to understand culture (*civilisations*) as deriving from the economy, demography and social structure, and of being comprehensible in the same way 'by means of statistical analysis, the

---

[31] Thompson 1951: 461. [32] Grimm 1819. [33] Deslongchamps 1838.
[34] Deslongchamps 1838, quoted in Thompson 1951: 377.
[35] Goody 1972; Goody and Gandah 1981, 2002.

play of structure and conjuncture and considerations of long term change rather than of events'.[36] Of statistics he says their interpretation can be very different depending upon the writer. Culture, he claims, requires a different treatment. Unlike the data of economics and social history, 'cultural objects are not manufactured by the historian but by the people he studies'. Of course, the same could be said of any other object of historical or anthropological enquiry, though not of their analysis, cultural, social or of whatever kind. And while numerical analysis may or may not be part of the actor's understanding of the situation (for sports fans it often is), it can be useful in comprehending the total situation in which meaning to the actor is part of meaning to the observer but does not represent the total range of his or her interests.

In this discussion Darnton's position seems to derive from a Geertzian approach coming in turn from that of Talcott Parsons, which allocates the social and the cultural to different subsystems with different specialists (sociologists in one case, studying 'structures', and anthropologists in the other, studying 'meaning') using different methods. That is not the situation for most European social scientists, for whom the Weberian or Durkheimian categories of social would include the cultural, though this is perhaps made clearer by the term sociocultural.

Writing of the relations between history and anthropology, Darnton cites Geertz, Turner, Rosaldo as well as Keith Thomas and Evans-Pritchard, but he does not refer to the more 'socially' orientated anthropologists involved in this rapprochement – a number of Americans (Wolf, Mintz), some of the English founding fathers of structural–functional analysis (Schapera, Gluckman, later those influenced by Marx such as Gough and Worsley), those interested in demographic and other history such as Macfarlane, nor the many other French anthropologists, again often touched by Marxist thinking. And were not Hobsbawm and Thompson among the first historians to probe the connection? But to consider these authors would have led towards the integration of the cultural, the social and the economic, rather than to their autonomy.

Darnton is firmly committed to understanding the specific event by means of 'thick description' and thereby comprehending the

---

[36] Darnton 1984: 257.

'mentality' of the actors. It is a rich vein which he rightly exploits, following Geertz's anthropological example. But it seems unwise to reject other approaches to understanding the past or the present, for example, that of looking at particular events in terms of the *longue durée* as well as of the short, and at the wider social structure in which the community is placed. One sees tendencies towards such approaches in Darnton's work and at times wishes they were more explicit, especially at the level of mentalities, which presents many difficulties.[37]

We should certainly explore the text in depth, as Darnton has done in a very fruitful way. But equally we have to take into account the social context of folktales. Who are the folk? And secondly we have to have some notion of the *longue durée* in terms of cultural history. To think that folktales of the Perrault type were ever the staple of adult discourse is not only counterintuitive, and not I suggest supported by the evidence, but is also to make assumptions about changes in mentalities, about the alien nature of the (eighteenth-century) past, that seems to disparage its members, and especially the peasants, drawing too close an analogy with the treatment of 'primitive' cultures where already the assumption needs to be questioned. Not that peasants and others did not have recourse to elements of belief (folk belief, if you will) that bore a close resemblance to those found in other cultures and which Frazer and his colleagues would have treated as 'survivals'. That is a different matter. But in any case, to treat such features as offering a window on a total 'mentality' seems a questionable procedure.[38] It is part of it, no doubt, just as the Oklahoma killings or school shootings are part of the American mentality or culture, but it would be highly dubious to take them as 'keys' to unlock understanding of the whole in the manner of the Balinese cockfight.

---

[37] See Lloyd 1990.
[38] One of the problems here is using language as a model for the whole of culture, as anthropologists frequently do.

CHAPTER 6

Animals, humans and gods
in northern Ghana

The societies of the decentralized, tribal LoDagaa ('acephalous') and the highly organized state of the Gonja live in similar surroundings and have a similar set of folktales as far as the three main categories of humans, gods and animals are concerned. But the proportion is different: more chiefs appear in the folktales of the non-centralized society, fewer in those of the centralized one. This is relevant to both the functional and the structural points of view, and speaks to the significance of cross-cultural communication and the role of 'fancy'.

In many respects LoDagaa and Gonja societies were very different, though both were situated in the savannah of northern Ghana. One was an acephalous, farming society with no regular political organization; chiefship was absent, though undoubtedly men of influence reached positions of leadership from time to time; there was no literate tradition and contact with Islam was very slight. Gonja on the other hand was a long-established, highly differentiated chiefdom, members of which kept up continuing contacts with northern Nigeria, the Niger bend and even the Mediterranean. The kingdom comprised a number of ethnic communities. Part of the population were Muslims, a few of these were literate and the whole society was influenced by the Islamic world in one respect or another.

But when we come to examine their folktales, there is a remarkable similarity in range and subject matters.[1] In this chapter I look only at the characters that appear in stories which have been collected among the LoDagaa (1950–2) and the Gonja (1956–7, 1964–6)

---

[1] I use the word 'oral narrative' in order to get round the problem of distinguishing between myth and folktale; by and large these might be considered nearer the second of these poles and I shall sometimes refer to them as such.

respectively.[2] I am fully aware of the limitations of what I am doing; clearly a more sophisticated thematic analysis should be applied to the same material. But much of the treatment of oral literature, of myth as of folktale, suffers from a poverty of data, inadequate recording, a lack of linguistic knowledge (which by some writers is even treated as an advantage), an ignorance of the context of recitation and a confusion between frames of reference and of explanation. There are few fields, in my opinion, where the canons of enquiry are so poorly applied, a situation which goes some way towards preserving the mystery of myth. Something can be done to rectify the situation by analysing a collection of tales gathered by the commentator in a simple and straightforward manner, since the results may have a wider significance.

The characters have been divided into humans, gods and animals. The boundaries of these categories are not altogether rigid, for the following reasons:

(i) While the Gonja and the LoDagaa place humans and animals in separate categories, there is no overall term for 'supernatural beings'. There are rather a number of groups whom we, as outsiders, might designate as supernatural, and whose characteristics may approach those of humans, of animals, or indeed of natural objects. The Earth clearly comes close to the latter; so does the Rain, although this word is etymologically linked to that for the High God among the Gonja (and associated with 'god' among the LoDagaa).[3] Again, ghosts are near to humans, having many of the characteristics of both.[4]

(ii) Gods, animals and humans interact in the same stories, few of which are confined to one category of being alone. For this to happen in a narrative context, communication has to take place between them. For this reason, all have to speak the language of humans, and behave in ways that are broadly understood by them.

---

[2] The first collection was made by me, the second in collaboration with Esther Newcomb Goody.

[3] Among the LoDagaa God/god is etymologically linked to the Sun; in both societies the actors deny the etymological association.

[4] See Lang 1893: xii: 'Among savages ... the characters were far more frequently *animals* than in European *Märchen* ... The gods are beasts or birds.'

(iii) The actors are not fixed eternally in these major categories; humans become ancestors and more complex transformations can always take place between them.[5] The rule and direction of these transformations are being studied.

ANIMALS

Among the LoDagaa, only the spider (*salminder*) occurs in more than a quarter of the stories (30 per cent); many other domestic and wild animals participate (see Tables 1 and 3[6]). In Gonja, spider stories are again the most numerous (36 per cent), followed by the hyena and the buffalo, then by much the same sort of range as among the LoDagaa (see Tables 2 and 3). The predominance of the spider is of course a feature of the West African scene, and the transportation of the Ananse stories of the Asante to the West Indies is well known. He is a typical trickster character, sometimes losing, sometimes winning, and the tales told about him frequently have a didactic ending.

HUMANS

The similarity between LoDagaa and Gonja is repeated with respect to humans. Here the similarity is even more surprising. Nature is much the same in both groups, especially with regard to wild and domestic animals, since they live in the West African savannah. But the social system differs, especially with regard to the political institutions: the Gonja had a traditional state, the LoDagaa acquired chiefs when they acquired the British, that is, about forty years before I collected these stories. So it is surprising to find that of all roles it is that of chief which stands out in both groups of stories. Yet more surprising is the fact that among the formerly non-centralized LoDagaa, there is an even higher percentage of such stories (15 per cent) than in the former kingdom of Gonja (8 per cent). Otherwise the narratives concern anonymous men/fathers or women/mothers (Tables 4, 5 and 6); overall rather a limited range of characters or roles is distinguished. Virtually no personal names are given.[7] Apart from chiefs,

---

[5] Goody 1972: 63; Stith Thompson 1955–8.
[6] These tables are given in the Appendix.
[7] Lang contrasts folktale and epic with respect to their anonymity (1893: xii).

the only difference between the two groups is the higher proportion of hunters and lepers that appear in the LoDagaa stories; again this difference has little counterpart in social life itself.

The reversal of the expected association with regard to chiefs has a parallel in the animal characters. While animals of the wild (LD, *wedun*), who form the main body of the *dramatis personae* in both groups of stories, are very similar, there is a slight difference among animals of the house (LD, *yirdun*). The most important of the domestic animals from the standpoint of consumption, that is, the cow, appears in none of the stories, although its wild counterpart, the bush-cow or buffalo, is well represented. The horse and the donkey appear in the stories of both groups, even though the activities associated with them (conquest in the case of the horse, trade in the case of the donkey) are found among the Gonja, not the LoDagaa. Indeed, as with the chief, horses appear slightly more frequently in the narratives of the society where they are most rare; they are found in 4 per cent of LoDagaa tales, and in 2 per cent of Gonja ones (Table 3).

The difference frequencies in the animals are slight, but it becomes more significant when viewed beside the similar reversal with respect to chiefs.

GODS

Not only do the Gonja have a very different political system than the LoDagaa, but the religions too are in many respects far apart. An important section of Gonja society is Muslim and the trading town of Salaga was a centre of Islamic learning, where its own literary 'school' flourished in the latter part of the nineteenth century. The influence of holy writ and of Islamic practice extended far outside the Muslim estate and many of the national ceremonies are based upon a religious calendar which celebrates phases in the life of Muhammad.

Consequently, God (that is, the Chief or High God, *Ewurabore*)[8] played a central role in Gonja, though other supernatural agencies also had an important place. Among the LoDagaa, on the other hand, God (*Na'angmin*) played little part in religious action; his role was that of

---

[8] In Gonja this particular usage is largely confined to the stories; in ordinary speech *bore* alone is used.

a remote being largely removed from everyday life, one of the 'otiose High Gods' found throughout Africa. Despite this difference in religious action and belief, the stories display a remarkable similarity both in the range of supernatural beings and in the frequency with which they appear. In both groups, the high God appears more than any other agency, the percentage being roughly the same, if one includes God's son among the LoDagaa (Tables 7, 8 and 9). But the second notable feature is that, apart from God, the only other beings mentioned are the 'fairies' (or beings of the wild) and ghosts (that is, ex-humans).

The 'beings of the wild' (or hill and water sprites, dwarfs, *genii* or fairies, as they are variously known in the literature) play an intermediary role between God and humans. As we have seen, they have an important part in the ritual activities of the LoDagaa and other societies in the region because, among other things, they are closely involved with the processes of communication between humans and other powers, especially in the process of divination. But on the day-to-day level other agencies such as the Earth and ancestors, not to mention the innumerable 'medicine shrines', play a greater part in religious action. Yet none of these are mentioned in the extensive sample of tales we have collected.

One further point concerns the interaction between the different categories of being. Table 10 in the Appendix shows that the most common type of narrative involves humans and animals. The next most frequent combination is that in which only humans or only animals appear; among the Gonja it is the latter that predominate, among the LoDagaa, the former. Again this appears to run counter to expectations based upon the rest of the sociocultural system, for Gonja society is perhaps less concerned with animals, more with managing people. Stories involving gods alone do not occur and even those where gods interact with other categories are few. Basically these stories are to do with animals and humans, more usually with the interaction of both. They are concerned with the natural rather than the supernatural world, and the boundary between 'nature' and 'culture' is of little importance here (indeed, I would argue the categories themselves do not exist in the actor frame of reference); humans become animals and vice versa. But, except as a ghost, human is not transformed to god, although god may change temporarily to animal or human.

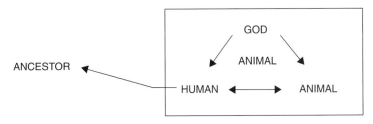

The problems arising out of the distribution of characters are threefold. Firstly, the characters in the narrative of these two societies are similar in a general way (as also seems to be the case with the plots, though the evidence is not presented here). Secondly, the small differences that exist contradict the structure of the societies; there is more of God and more of chiefs in the pagan, acephalous group. Thirdly, the selection of characters in both societies concentrates upon a limited and in some respects atypical segment of the total roles available to human beings and to supernatural agencies.

Though the explanations we suggest for these problems are linked together, we will take them one by one. Firstly, the similarity in the range of characters and in the stories themselves indicates their relative independence from other sociocultural variables. Only in a very limited way are the stories specific to the culture of any one society in the area. Instead they form part of a pool of narratives which circulate over a geographical region, like novels in western society today and folktales in days gone by.

The process by which they do so is understandable if one considers the context in which they are recited and transmitted. Unlike the long Bagre recitation of the LoDagaa or certain Muslim stories of the Gonja, both of which might be regarded as lying at the mythical end of the narrative continuum, these tales are not associated with any particular occasion, ritual or secular. They are told in a variety of circumstances, but mainly to and often by children. Most of the tales in our collection were recorded by the young and the contexts in which they were normally told was when a group of children were sitting together in the evening. Some adults did act as storytellers, but usually when children had already started a 'round' of tales and the grown-ups would join in to show what they could do. Invariably they were acting in a special manner, recognizing that they had not altogether put away childish things.

This fact had some profound implications for the analysis of the characteristics of the *pensée sauvage* which has been little appreciated. In her study of the tales relating to the origin of death, Paulme quotes one of Cardinall's collection from Togoland, which refers to the area between Krachi and Salaga. Experience of this relatively sophisticated part of the world (Krachi harboured a scholar whose translations of pre-Islamic poetry amazed the anthropologist-administrator Rattray) makes me wonder whether any adult 'believed' stories of this kind. I myself have always heard them told in a lighthearted way and generally to children. Paulme herself describes the Bete equivalents as 'laughing-tales', which is their own name, and she remarks that the storyteller's main concern is with his audience.[9] If this is so, then to use such stories for the analysis of 'primitive thought' (as she did) may be not too far removed from using the gooseberry bush and stork stories for the analysis of European concepts of the universe, or anyhow of their views on conception. The statement is more obviously true of the overt content of narrative; but, if the concepts involved are of any significance, it must also hold for the more cryptophoric analyses of hidden meaning, of 'deep structure', however this should be arrived at.

The problem here is partly one of levels of thought. Adults may have different levels of interpretation for communicating among themselves. For communicating with children they may adopt a less complex mode, one which stresses a simplified form of explanation. One of the reasons for this is that children everywhere (but in different degrees) demand explanations for the phenomena they encounter; they ask questions, like 'what does God look like?', that adults would rarely ask and never answer. It seems likely that in many such contexts people place field enquirers in the same category as children. In the first place, their understanding of the language is often limited; in the second, they tend to ask the disconcerting question ('what is the soul?') that adults have long since set aside as impossible to answer. In these areas the replies they get are likely to resemble those given to children, since these are the only ones

⁹ Paulme 1967: 58–9.

available to meet direct challenges of this kind. But whether they are analysing definite folktales or their own fragmentary fieldnotes, enquirers stand in grave danger of taking for 'primitive belief' the conceptual simplifications that, as we have seen, characterize communications with children or that mark the lighthearted occasion. This is not true of the more serious, more sacred tale, which we often call myth (though many use the term in an all-embracing way), but it reminds us that a determination of the context of communication must be a precursor of any serious analysis of oral forms.

I have yet to deal with the problem of similar tales in dissimilar social systems. Given the context of recital, the storyteller is sometimes searching for a new twist to an old tale, sometimes for a new tale. This is especially true when the audience is youthful or the occasion lighthearted. At the present time in northern Ghana, one can easily observe the very rapid circulation of songs and dances among adolescents throughout the region, though some remain characteristic of particular groups. The same is true of narratives, as we have mentioned in Chapter 2 on oral literature. The source is often irrelevant provided the tale is meaningful, and meaning here relates to general human elements rather than to culturally specific ones. Hence borrowing is very frequent; a person may hear a tale in the market and go back to repeat it in his own village. Indeed, what happens is not really a case of borrowing or diffusion, since all draw from the same pool, though modifying the stories as they do so. This situation is confirmed by Paulme for the Bete of the Ivory Coast; she writes:

After my return to Paris I went through tales from Mali, Guinea and other parts of Africa and was not very surprised to see that *practically every one of my Bete tales had already been noted elsewhere*, although some were told in quite a different way. The position was thus of a pattern which is roughly the same everywhere but which the teller, consciously or not, modifies. His concern is with his audience, '*whose attention he must keep*'.[10]

Indeed, versions of some of these stories are common in the Mediterranean world and appear in collections such as the *Thousand and One Nights*. The phenomenon is one with which we are quite familiar in Europe from the work of many scholars of the folk

[10] Paulme 1967: 58–9, my italics.

tradition, though they have given little attention to the context of transmission.

If these stories are not specific to particular situations and are primarily directed to a youthful or lighthearted audience, then it becomes clear why they are similar over large geographical areas and among different tribal groups. It is this larger than 'tribal' reference that creates a uniformity of characterization in any one place. Chiefs are found in both LoDagaa and Gonja stories, though more or less only in Gonja society. Let me point out here that while the LoDagaa did not have chiefs in the usual sense (though they have acquired them with the British), they did know about the chiefly societies of the region (as well as having rich men, sometimes known as 'chiefs'), especially those that formerly raided them for slaves. The models of acephaly and state were present to them, but, unlike the Kachin of Burma, such societies moved towards the centralized pole mainly as the result of conquest.[11] Consequently, they can well understand the role of chiefs in society; indeed, they are more attracted by stories about such characters than the centralized Gonja, with their long history of state organization.

This situation might seem to be a case of the myth reversing the actuality. But, with this formula, as with certain others, everything and therefore nothing is explained.[12] Why reverse here and not elsewhere? I do not myself see any great significance in this reversal; the modification and selection of stories may certainly reflect a particular sociocultural system, but the present differences seem to result from arresting the gene-pool of stories that flows through the whole area at a particular time.

The third problem I raised had to do with the choice of characters. Although the range of animals is extensive, human roles are very restricted. Supernatural ones are even more so; virtually the only agencies represented are God and the beings of the wild. One could try to explain this selection by referring to the circulation of tales with these constituting the common element among all the societies. Such a suggestion has little to recommend it since, over the region as a whole, the Earth and the ancestors are more important than God, and the diviner was certainly more widespread than the chief.

---

[11] There was possibly a limited oscillation as the result of internal pressures.
[12] Lévi-Strauss 1968: 207–8.

Moreover, it is significant that in the long LoDagaa myth associated with the Bagre society, the same supernatural agencies dominate the plot, God and the beings of the wild. If one were to use the Bagre as a key to LoDagaa religion (and many writers have gone further and used less elaborate and more shadowy tales as keys to unlock the whole cultural system), it would open the door upon a very narrow segment of the ritual and mystical field. Any interpretation of LoDagaa society based upon the myth would be partial, more so than trying to understand the society of Homer's own time from the content of the *Odyssey* and the *Iliad*.

One major aspect of the Bagre myth, I have argued, was 'explanatory'; that is, an effort is made to explain the origin of man and his culture.[13] As a result a special emphasis was placed upon God (the final cause) and upon those beings who acted as intermediaries between gods and men. The theocentric character of the First Bagre is related to its aetiological role.

It was precisely this aetiological aspect of myth that Malinowski rejected in favour of a functional approach, which tended to set aside the 'belief element'. The recent treatment of myth has laid more stress on speculation, as we have recently been reminded, but it is the speculation of the observer rather than the actor. Structural interpretations are often more concerned to explain away than to explain. For Lévi-Strauss, myth, at its face value, is arbitrary and he dismisses alternative explanations of myth as 'reducing mythology either to idle play or to a crude kind of philosophic speculation'.[14] Both these approaches, the 'functional' and 'structural', often seem to be ways of explaining away the 'irrational'. My own view is different; oral narrative, whether myth, legend or folktale, has many functions and many levels of interpretation. But when discussing creation, people are (among other things) demanding or providing an explanation. Since creation was a unique event, they look to the unitary facet of the supernatural – namely God.[15] In the human context, they also look towards the head, the chief, as representative of the human situation.

Folktales are not explanatory in the same way as the Bagre myth. My contention is that they are largely directed towards the young

[13] See my introduction to *The Myth of the Bagre* (Oxford: Clarendon Press, 1972).
[14] Lévi-Strauss 1968: 297.
[15] See my review of G. S. Kirk, *Myth in Ancient Cultures*, *Times Literary Supplement*, 14 August 1970.

and those who need to be entertained. Nevertheless, in some tales a didactic element is visible in the moral tacked on at the end, and often only tenuously derived from the story. The explanatory element is equally visible in other stories, for example, those about the origin of death as well as in many of the spider tales. This emphasis tends to place in primary focus those characters who stand as the *fons et origo* of their different domains, that is, the chief for men, God for gods and (in a different sense) the spider for the animals. The selection of characters and the imposition of a hierarchical structure derive more from the context of communication than the nature of the polity.

CONCLUSION

In this discussion of LoDagaa and Gonja folktales, a well-defined genre in West Africa as a whole, the question is raised as to why the beings that appear in them (animals, humans and gods) are so similar, despite the great dissimilarities in the societies themselves. I argue that they form part of a pool of stories, told largely for entertainment (mainly for the young), which circulate throughout the region with only minimal adaptation to local societies; their appeal lies on a much more general level.

Regarding the selection of the characters, I asked why the chief and God should be the main characters, even where otherwise little attention was paid to them. This choice is partly because the stories are drawn from the pool, but partly too because of their aetiological aspects, which offer some kind of explanation of the human situation, but directed to a young audience or one ready to be entertained. Not only entertained, because there is some evidence that children first believe in the 'truth' of such stories until life (or adults) disillusions them, that they are really 'fairy' stories. An explanation for this apparent reversal has to do with the knowledge people had in acephalous societies of chiefly ones, which they were always considering as the chiefly ones descended on them from time to time with their horses and their guns to seek slaves, grain and anything else they could carry with them. Acephalous groups were rightly afraid of such chiefly groups, but also there was the free-floating nature of folktales that left little time or space for adaptation.

CHAPTER 7

The Bagre in all its variety

The types (genre) of oral literature are many, but they differ in significant ways from written forms. 'Myth', for example, is seen as a typical oral form. So it is because we define it that way. But it is much more variable than much current theorizing allows, which has complicating implications for its analysis.

The Bagre is the name of a 'secret' association found among the LoDagaa of north-west Ghana and in neighbouring communities. Together with my late friend, Kum Gandah, I have published three volumes containing the transcription and translation of the long work that is recited in the course of the complex initiation recitals in the settlement of Birifu. The first was called *The Myth of the Bagre* (1972), the second, translated into French as well as English, *Une recitation du Bagré* (1981). The third contains further transcription and translations, especially from other settlements, the parishes of Gomble and Biro, which are 'under' Birifu where the other versions were recorded, but mainly from Lawra situated some ten miles away, which preserves most of the ritual but offers a very different 'myth' to accompany it.

To understand the recitation, one needs some knowledge of the association, the accompanying rituals and to some extent the society itself. These I will provide briefly. But I want to begin by saying something about the importance of this recitation for the study of 'myth', for the study of standardized oral forms ('oral literature'), for the elucidation of 'primitive thought' and for the comparative study of cognitive processes such as memory.

The 'Myth of the Bagre' is the long recitation, in rhythmic speech, and in 1949 I recorded a version by dictation from Benima Dagarti outside the ritual setting; inside would obviously have been impossible before the advent of portable audio-recorders, a fact well worth remembering when considering earlier versions of oral performance. It took me some ten days to write down and many years to annotate and translate, first with the aid of assistants in the locality, and especially in the later stages helped by S. W. D. K. (Kum) Gandah, a teacher, entrepreneur and politician, from the same settlement of Birifu, who had come to England in the 1960s as the result of political difficulties, and with whom I later collaborated on further versions. That first version was published by Clarendon Press, Oxford, in 1972.

Meanwhile, Gandah and I returned in 1970 with the aim of recording a version in the process of being actually recited, this time with a portable audio recorder. But it was not the right time of the year for the ceremonies and my companion had to persuade his Nayiili lineage, with a few other kinsfolk, to perform outside the chief's house. I myself could not approach too closely because of my uninitiated status, but I installed myself in a hut nearby, where I operated the audio recorder and made notes. That is the recitation we published in Paris in *Classiques africaines*.[1] This recital included another version of the White, the Black and the Funeral Bagre, which should only be performed at the death of a member. Its presentation on this occasion aroused doubts in the minds of some and subsequent misfortunes were attributed to this performance. The only recordings made in the context of an actual ceremonial performance are the versions published in the Third Bagre volume and recorded in Ngmanbili, Gomble, Biro and Lawra.

One of these was from a central part of Birifu where the previous versions came from; that is, the Ngmanbili (White) performance. Then there is one White and one Black performance from a parish on the outskirts of Birifu, namely Gomble, and a further version of the Black from the neighbouring parish of Biro, which was recited a few days later by the same Speaker but which is substantially shorter (1,646 lines compared with 2,781). A very different series of recordings came from the local administrative centre of Lawra, situated some ten miles to the north of Birifu. There a similar sequence of ceremonies was performed, with more or less the same gestures and

---

[1] Goody and Gandah 1981.

significances. But here we recorded not simply the main recitations but all the verbal interaction that went on while the rituals were being performed and also those leading up to them. Some of this transcription may seem inconsequential, even noise, but it gives a firsthand idea of what takes place at such performances and how these are organized. The recordings include the recitation of the White Bagre, much reduced compared with the Birifu versions; the Black is virtually absent, partly I believe due to the failure of our machinery. But they also include a long legend of how the clan organizing the performances, the Kusiele patriclan, arrived in the area and why and how it began to perform the Bagre. This legend is recited both in prose and in verse – that is, in the short rhythmic phrase I transcribe as 'lines', each of which has one or two strongly stressed syllables and is often marked by the beating of a stick on wood.

Why should we consider the Bagre important for social science and for the humanities generally? The first point has to do with the nature of 'culture' in this and other oral societies. For the recordings show how great a measure of variation can exist in such performances; not in all their facets but in the case of long recitations I would be prepared to say 'has to exist'. That idea knocks on the head any question of such works (myths is one name used for them) being taken as a foundation 'text' for a particular social order since they are always plural and the variation between the versions is very considerable. What happens is negotiated publicly and what is recited is worked out verbally, using imagination. Look in this case at the difference between the Lawra Bagre and the Birifu Bagre. Both can be assumed to have emerged from one common ancestor, yet the subsequent divergence has been radical, in orientation as well as in content and length. In one case the stress is on a cosmological account, in the other on a migration story, each embodying quite different quests of origin. Long recitations are certainly not the only form of cultural activity that displays such a range of variation. Even the rituals of Bagre, which offer more continuity, show some significant changes between Birifu and Lawra. Such variations have been concealed because most fieldwork in oral cultures, even intensive fieldwork, takes place over a short period and in a limited area. Temporal changes of this kind are either ignored or seen in relation to long-term 'social change' rather than as a regular feature of oral cultures which are consequently conceived as more rule-bound, more conforming, more traditional, hence less inventive, than they actually are. I return to this notion of traditional when discussing sociological concepts of modernity.

There is a particular problem for analysis raised by this aspect of the Bagre. It is often assumed that a recorded version of an oral myth stands in the same relationship to the society that produced it as the Old Testament did to ancient Hebrew society, rather as the Myth and Ritual school assumed there was a direct and unique relationship between the two. It is on that basis that much discussion of 'myth' (in the sense of long oral recitation of a cosmological kind) has taken place. But directly we see that these forms vary so greatly, and not, I submit, around a determinative core but rather as a syntagmatic chain, the problem takes on a different character. We can no longer see, as Lévi-Strauss did in his monumental studies of South American mythology, a single recitation as a unique key to the interpretation of a culture. The myth unlocks no single door as it exists in the plural, changing radically over time. It is obviously one part of culture but hardly a key to the whole. That at least is the case with the Bagre. The first part which discusses ritual (the White Bagre) remains relatively the same in these various versions. As I have remarked elsewhere, the order of the ceremonies is something that participants do tend to remember 'by heart'. One leads to another as Christmas does to Epiphany, and that in turn to Easter. Occasionally people make a mistake in the sequence but they are soon corrected. That sequence is central to the White Bagre, which consists essentially of an outline and very partial account of what has to be done at varying intervals at each of the ceremonies that take place. The account is elaborated differently in each version, and in the First Bagre it is much more extensive, including a version of the story of how the younger brother was led to begin to perform the Bagre as well as some theoretical discussion about the role of various supernatural agencies, including God himself, in the scheme of things. Its length was 6,133 lines compared with 1,204 in the version from Gomble.

The more speculative, philosophical, Black Bagre, changes much more radically. How radically we see from the Lawra Bagre, in the course of which all these other recordings were made and indeed performed by members of the same clan as the Gomble Bagre in Birifu.

But here the recitations are very different and the Black has in effect been replaced by a clan legend or 'history', what I call the Coming of the Kusiele, of which we find no parallel in Birifu. Yet the local population see it all as the same ritual and recitation, the Bagre, and can attend each other's performances as full members. However, the differences are enormous, as we can see from the text and translation. For earlier scholars that version in the First Bagre would have been the only one in (recorded) existence and could easily have been taken as paradigmatic. Indeed, that was the case with that first version when it was published, at least by some literate members of the LoDagaa themselves. However, the further recordings and transcriptions show that in fact it cannot be understood in this way. In my fieldwork I might have first come across and published a very different version than the one I did. Yet how often has this possibility been ignored in parallel cases when we are dealing with the rather limited material (compared with the potential that is available) recorded from oral cultures? That was a problem that could be overlooked with the earlier techniques of recording but has changed radically with the electronic age.

That conservation raises a further analytical problem. I have distinguished between myths as specific recitations and mythologies which are not found as such as a cultural form but are pieced together by observers (and occasionally by actors) from statements about a particular cosmology from a variety of sources. This enterprise presumes that one can extract a common set of ideas from an undefined range of cultural interactions, from recitations, songs, everyday speech and from the replies to the enquirer's queries. But if variation in belief is as wide as a study of the Bagre suggests, such a procedure must be highly dangerous and misleading. One cannot add up the different notions of God, or of creation, at any moment and come out with a single adequate statement for all time.

The same would be true of music, both of song and of the tune played on the xylophone, which often takes the form of thematic elaboration of an old song or the composition of an invented one. In the absence of a literate notation there is no process of composition in the western sense. But there is invention and there is change. Of course there are songs as in the Bagre that have to be repeated at every performance, although one may doubt whether they are performed

and sung in exactly the same way each time – the degree of variation could only be ascertained by careful recording and analysis. But
from the standpoint of the authors they are the same song and my
informal observations suggest that a large measure of identity exists.
That is not true of much of the xylophone music that accompanies
the dance. The player will make up, adapt or borrow a song and then
elaborate variations over a period of fifteen minutes or more. In these
recitals, invention takes an important place and there is no question
of repetition being valued for its own sake, as many concepts of the
traditional would suggest.

This problem about 'myth' is one to which J. L. Siran draws
attention in his illuminating booklet, *L'Illusion mythique*.[2] He points
out that for the Dogon, the prototypical West African society studied by Griaule and his associates in France, there is no *récit*, no
standardized oral form, but the so-called 'myth' consists of a cosmology constructed by the (anthropological) observer(s). That is
the difference between what I have hesitatingly called 'the Myth
of the Bagre' among the LoDagaa and the myth of the Dogon as
recounted by the anthropologists. Mine is a straight translation,
theirs a construction.

Siran thinks that the notion of recitation presumes a reading from
a written text; hence he objects to my term for the Bagre. It is true
that the term *may* presume a text, as when one recites a poem by
Baudelaire. But that notion is not intrinsic to the usage, at least in
English. In French too *récit* can include any narrative whether there
is a written text or not. Even in the absence of such a writing, some
authors have also used the notion of *texte* with regard to oral narratives and cultural performances in general. For me that is thoroughly
confusing because although people have precedents, such a usage
assimilates oral production too closely to the model of the fixed form
in written cultures. There is an enormous degree of invention and
elaboration as well as memorization in the Bagre, and I would argue
in any long form (*genre*) of this kind. While one usage of recitation
would be inappropriate, I do not see that, reverting to *récit*, another
is not perfectly suitable; indeed Siran himself uses the word *récit* in
this sense on many occasions.

[2] Siran 1998.

Siran further objects that the Dogon have no category term (genre name) for their 'myth'. Neither have the LoDagaa, even though it is an actual standardized form. One would hardly expect such a name to exist in any language where almost by definition there is only one instance in any particular culture. It is the same for the Bagre, which is certainly not an *aserkpang*, a story, tale; and it is the same for the Bible or for any other holy book seen as the word of God. However, it does not seem inappropriate for observers to provide a category term if they perceive similarities across cultures and this is what we (not only anthropologists) do very frequently. That a society of humans (or of butterflies) has no ethnocategory is a relevant but not determining factor for instituting such a concept. It is for this reason that I use the word 'myth' to describe the recitation known as the Bagre in order to draw attention to the very general similarities with other long cosmological recitations, like that of the Zuni of North America.

Siran has a third objection to the word myth and this occupies the major part of his book. It refers to the same general point that I made in Chapter 1, 'Religion and ritual from Tylor to Parsons: the definitional problem',[3] and that arose out of my work on LoDagaa funerals. I regarded the usage of the word 'ritual' as indicating acts for which observers had no 'rational' explanation in terms of their accepted means–end relationships, in terms, that is, of their own worldview or orientation. Siran makes a similar point about 'myth' and 'mythical', which he rightly claims are used to describe the beliefs of others to which we don't subscribe, excluding from the category even our own account of the supernatural, as in the Bible. Clearly that position is unsustainable. But I would not go so far as to include in this objection our 'scientific' beliefs, which seem to me of a different order. Firstly, they set aside the supernatural element; they are secular, non-transcendental. Secondly, they are subject to continual scrutiny, to confirmation and disconfirmation, in the manner discussed by Kuhn[4] for Europe and by Lloyd[5] for ancient Greece. Parallel techno-scientific procedures exist in other cultures, as Malinowski insisted for the Trobriands, but they are not given the same cultural prominence, universality or explicit experimental validation. Notions

---

[3] Originally Goody 1961.   [4] Kuhn 1962.   [5] Lloyd 1991.

of proof, to follow Lloyd's usage, are part of cultural history and develop significantly with writing; they are not static over the long term and these become institutionalized with the Renaissance.[6]

Siran is quite correct in refusing to characterize the thought (mentality) of oral cultures, of 'simple societies', as mythical or mytheopoeic, as distinct from 'scientific' or indeed 'rational' (as others have proclaimed). If there is a difference, it cannot be phrased in these terms, since both coexist (though in different degrees). However, he places the difference, for example, between Europe and South America at another level altogether, at that of underlying schemata as between the flying (/Vol-/) of the latter and the look (/Regard-/) of the former. These schemata are a priori for each individual, and for Durkheim constitute the fundamental categories of the understanding that originated in society. Exactly how was never clear.

The question that remains is the scope and binding (or organizing) nature of these schemata. If they encapsulate differences, are those differences related (as some earlier ones have certainly been) to differences in scientific and technological achievements? While we can agree with Malinowski (and Siran) that both these types of activity are always present, they are clearly present to different degrees; there have been cumulative developments in forms of proof (or disproof) and forms of experimentation. These seem to me differences with which any history of culture has to engage, but not at the level of mentalities, of fixed patterns of thought, rather of the presence or absence of certain of what I have called 'technologies of the intellect' and their consequences. As I have insisted, that does not imply a Great Divide but it allows for a plurality of developmental changes in, *inter alia*, the means and mode of communication.

The most general problem for the social sciences raised by the Bagre material pertains to this last point. Much sociological thinking, today and in the past, is based around the contrast between the traditional and the modern, as in the work of Max Weber and in the assumptions of most sociologists since his day. Traditional societies were marked by custom and were relatively static, following precedent automatically rather than working things out 'rationally'. Such views were given a more specifically anthropological slant in

---

[6] Goody 2009.

the writings of Lévy-Bruhl, as in *The Soul of the Primitive*.[7] I do not wish to question the fact that the rhythm of social change, especially technological and scientific change, has increased enormously in the last four hundred years. But that the simpler societies were static, did not act 'reflexively' as the current jargon has it, thinking of reflexivity as a feature of modernity and not of tradition, that notion has to be set completely on one side (at least as far as religion is concerned) when we look at the variations in the recitation of the Bagre. As I have argued, these are not simply verbal variants circulating around a permanent core, but include radical changes of philosophical attitude, for example, as between creationist and evolutionary perspectives on the origin of the world, or between theological and more materialist views of the creation of culture.[8]

Even written versions of oral work can produce extraordinarily different interpretations, as we see in the case of Braimah's recording of the Gonja drum history. In this case, however, one can go back to the 'original' version and the comments recorded by the drummer.[9] Here it is not so much a matter of different versions as of different interpretations of an archaic drum language and the writers' desire to make sense of their understanding.

The sociologist Anthony Giddens sees reflexivity as a characteristic of modernity,[10] as a breakthrough from tradition where what are largely face-to-face communities act in accordance with custom, with what has gone before. In making this claim the author takes up the long-established dichotomous view of tradition and modernity. Reflexivity means people think about the world and their position in it. According to this view, in pre-modern societies they do not. I argue that this notion of 'How Natives Think' is even cruder than the much-criticized approach of Lévy-Bruhl since it no longer enquires into differences but is based purely on the supposed absence of reflexivity, of thinking. Pre-moderns are seen not as active agents but as passive actors, who accept what culture hands down to them as tradition. That conception may be largely true of some elements of culture such as language, which necessarily changes only slowly – otherwise there would be little intergenerational understanding. Or

[7] Lévy-Bruhl 1928.   [8] Goody 1998.   [9] E. and J. Goody 1991.
[10] Giddens 1991: 20.

of earlier technology, agricultural for example, where it would be dangerous to set aside tried methods unless one was sure of the alternatives, otherwise the supply of food might suffer. It is much less true of ritual and even less true of 'myth' in the sense of long recitations which, as in the case of the Bagre, vary greatly over time and space, including in highly significant spheres like notions of the High God and of the creation of the world. In these and other areas, culture, precedent or even mental templates may lay down some vague parameters, but within these boundaries, individual reciters speculate about the nature of supernatural beings and their relation with the universe. They do not seem too constrained by past formulations of the problem.

In this way the example of the transmission of one cultural object, the Bagre, seems to say something about the transmission of information (of culture) more generally. In his provocative and stimulating book *Religion Explained*,[11] Pascal Boyer adapts the ideas of other, biologically inclined, scholars in his analysis of the communication of ideas and practices. Cultural transmission, he writes, 'could be to some extent described in the same way as genetic transmission'.[12] Following Dawkins he begins by seeing culture as a population of *memes* 'which are just "copy-me" programs, like genes'. They are units of culture such as stories 'that get people to speak or act in certain ways that make other people store a replicated version of these mental units … You hear them once, they get stored in memory, they lead to behaviours … that will implant copies … in other people's memories.'[13] This mechanical description of cultural tradition may even correspond to a description of some written religions (where there is always a template to reduce or call attention to any variation). But it is, I suggest, inadequate for the process whereby the Bagre is transmitted and where 'memory' is much more 'creative' and 'inventive'. So the idea of a template, whether structural, functional or genetic, is a good deal less persuasive.

In fact Boyer later rejects the notion of memes and of replication as misleading.[14] 'People's ideas are sometimes roughly similar to those of other people around them, not because ideas can be downloaded

---

[11] Boyer 2001.   [12] Boyer 2001: 34.   [13] Boyer 2001: 35.
[14] Boyer 2001: 40.

from mind to mind but because they are reconstructed in a similar way.' But he still retains the notion of templates, intuitions and inferences. Cultural material is consistently being reshuffled according to inferences which are 'governed by special principles in the mind' and therefore the results are 'predictable' and 'non-random'.[15] However, inferences are clearly less constraining than memes and lead to a freer reshuffling in terms of 'special principles' (undefined).

Culture in Boyer's eyes 'is the name of a similarity'.[16] That may well be true of the standard anthropological description of social interaction based on a short visit, which is nevertheless assumed to continue in the same (quasi-genetic) way over the centuries. It may also be the case with some aspects of 'tradition', which assume a static situation and a more or less exact 'handing over'. It may lie behind the discussion of national character, even in some versions of anthropological theory.[17] And certainly it may be more true of certain aspects of the social scene than of others, of agriculture, for example. But it cannot be considered correct for the transmission of the Bagre *over time*, nor is it correct for Barth's interesting description of religious and other concepts among the Baktaman of New Guinea.[18]

The advantage that Boyer sees fixed memes as having for humankind may be better accounted for in communicative terms, having little to do with a template. I pronounce English words the way I do so that I can communicate with my fellows, who correct my pronunciation, not because I am constrained biologically to speak in a particular way. It is always possible for me to move to France and to learn a quite different language for the same purpose. That form of acquisition is basically different from genetic transmission, although it goes without saying that any human behaviour must be 'compatible' with the genetic. That in the end is a rather weak statement. All human communication involves a measure of reflexivity but that is clearly much greater with writing, where what has been 'said' is reflected back on the reader, normally increasing the speed of cultural change. Except of course in religious discourse, where what is reflected back is not the evanescent word of human kind but the enduring word of God or his intermediaries.

---

[15] Boyer 2001: 42.   [16] Boyer 2001: 35.   [17] Darnton 1984.
[18] Barth 1987.

Later in his volume, Boyer recognizes that the account of memes does not allow for the wide variety of cultural forms that we find. On the other hand, he does not see people's concepts as in 'constant flux'.[19] Only some are subject to complex inferences, which tend to go in certain directions rather than others, depending upon their compatibility with mental templates; these items become part of what is handed down (tradition), the rest are discarded. Inferences often constitute a centrifugal force that makes representations 'diverge in unpredictable ways'. But in some domains, 'acting as a centripetal force, inferences and memories lead to roughly similar constructions even though the input may be quite different' 'because of a similar template'.[20] The notion of similarity and indeed universality is very important to rehabilitate in the social sciences and one that has often been neglected by current trends in cultural anthropology. But this account, while ingenious, seems vague, leaving many questions unanswered. My own emphasis, while not denying the possibility of 'templates', of preprogrammed ideas, would also see the universality of religious or other concepts as being more likely to originate in the confrontation of language-speaking humans with their environment. I have discussed this question at greater length in *Representations and Contradictions*.[21]

I imagine the 'initial situation' for religion as being one in which language-using primates are faced with the problem both of developing a system of sounds (phonology) and a system of representations and meaning about themselves and their environment. Humankind is forced to create verbal concepts in order to communicate. Whatever is there beforehand in terms of animate/inanimate distinctions and the like is of great simplicity compared with what now emerges in order to communicate about things, persons and actions in their absence by means of verbal representations. By virtue of the fact that they are never the thing itself, they always involve another level of reality, of conceptualization. The binary nature of certain of these concepts, as they have been perceived in structuralist terms, is related not so much to the binary nature of the mind and its templates as to the way in which in linguistic terms we perceive our bodies and designate the world in general. The alternative is to see templates such

---

[19] Boyer 2001: 45.   [20] Boyer 2001: 45.   [21] Goody 1997a.

as Boyer envisages developing in pre-language-using primates. But how do we develop biologically a template for tools (or even persons) when we have no such instruments for communication (or only in a very limited way)? Furthermore, what validation can there be for considering 'tools' as an 'ontological category', as he does, as distinct from looking at more concrete units? The difference between these levels could also be described in terms of degrees of abstraction, but here the more inclusive level is given a highly significant epithet of its own ('ontological') which seems to take the central assumptions for granted.

Boyer's theory of religion, culture and the mind presumes there is a core of stable notions that are selected because they correspond to intuitions derived from ontological categories. He sees such categories as being limited in number, Animal, Person, Tool, Natural Object and Plant ('more or less exhaust the lot'[22]). Ontological categories display a limited set of features some of which 'religion' violates (though the violations may be conceptual). Is that presumption of stability justified? I have argued against it both with regard to the Bagre recitations over the short term (e.g. in *Food and Love*) and regarding cultural history over the longer one (in *Representations and Contradictions*), seeing the changes in representations, here verbal, as almost inevitable, given the many possibilities for the selection of words and, at the level of ideas, given the contradictions that are inherent in the process of representation (which are never altogether what they seem) producing an ambivalence that leads to the oscillation, to the *va-et-vient* of ideas.

Let me now turn to the more detailed examination of the Bagre.

THE CONTEXT

The series of Bagre performances begins about August and continues at irregular intervals over the dry season; the rainy season is too occupied with farming. The first ceremony is the Announcement of Bagre (*Bag puoru*),[23] when the neophytes being proposed for membership are brought to the Bagre house, where the performance will later be carried out, the house of the 'Bagre mother'. They are brought there

---

[22] Boyer 2001: 78.   [23] Goody 1972.

by their sponsors, the 'Bagre fathers', who provide the malted grain and other contributions which the neophytes need to contribute. These initial contributions are then measured by the Bagre joking partners. When they say the word, the neophytes and their sponsors disperse, prepared to be called back for the next ceremony.

The recordings of ceremonies for the Third Bagre at Lawra begin with the Beating of the Malt. This is not the first of the ceremonies to take place, but it is the first at which we were present. In this case the recitation took place in the byre of the chief's house, he being head of this lineage of the Kusiele clan. What is recited there is considerably different from the White and the Black Bagre of Birifu, which are also recited here but in a much shorter form. It consists of a long recital in verse of 3,724 'lines' and is essentially a legend of how the ancestors of the clan arrived in their present location, how Kontol, son of Dafor, left the settlement of Babile, now an important market centre on the main road near Birifu some 10 miles south of Lawra, searching for farm land and general well-being.

> … to make it good
> for childbirth,
> for hunting
> and for raising chickens. (lines 442–5)

At line 1,307 the formula is repeated with farming now added. Kontol eventually came close to what is now Lawra where he found signs of buffalo so he knew there was water nearby. The soil was good and the area had even been settled by earlier inhabitants, the Janni, who had left for the right bank of the River Volta (now Burkina Faso) at the approach of the Kusiele, abandoning their ruined houses, grinding places and other items they could not move.

Kontol called his people, settled there, and the boundaries of the parish, the Earth shrine area, were laid out. But in order to succeed in childbirth, farming, hunting and raising livestock, he realized he had to perform the same rites, especially the Bagre, as his forefathers had done. In this way we are presented with an account of the sequence of the ceremonies such as we find in the White Bagre of Birifu (the First and Second Bagres, and the Gomble White in the Third volume). This account plays something of the same role as the Bagre of Birifu, because it tells of events leading up to the day's performance and then lists the ceremonies in the order in which they occur. It begins with the recitation up to the present performance of the Beating of the Malt. In this account of the Lawra Bagre, the Beating of the Malt (line 2,463)[24] is preceded by the Measuring of the Malt (line 2,001), then Bagre Greeting (line 2,355), the Yam Ceremony (line 2,367) and the Climbing of the Hill (line 2,438). It is followed by the Bagre Dance.

In the First Bagre of Birifu the sequence began with the Asperging of the Neophytes (*Bag puoru*, p. 64) and is followed by the Announcement (p. 66), which involves 'measuring the malt' and is sometimes combined with the Asperging, by the Ceremony of Beans (p. 76) shortly after which yams are eaten, by the Ceremony of the Bean Flower (p. 79), in some cases by the Beer of the Bagre Medicine (p. 81), the Whitening Ceremony (p. 81) and then the Beating of the Malt (p. 88), leading to the Bagre Dance (p. 92) followed by two shorter finalizing performances. The first two and the last two main ceremonies are obviously similar, even if the names do not show this. In the Second Bagre at Birifu, the Announcement of Bagre (line 2,241) includes 'the measuring of the malt', then the eating of yams (line 2,807), the Whitening Ceremony (line 2,823), the Ceremony of Beans (line 2,875), the Ceremony of the Bean Flower (line 2,948), the Beating of the Malt and the Bagre Dance (line 3,602). The differences in the ceremonies are much less than those in the recitation itself (especially the Black); members of different settlements can recognize what is happening but variation does occur.

PERSONNEL

When a neophyte passes out, he becomes a first grader, a White Bagre member (*Bo pla*). At a further ceremony, he will become a second grader, a Black Bagre member, who will have all the accoutrements as well as the medicine. If he himself sponsors a Bagre member, he becomes a Bagre father; if he sponsors the whole performance, using his house, he is the Bagre mother. The mother (always male) rates higher than the father. In addition there are the various Speakers who recite the Bagre, as well as the members who are asked to bring their

---

[24] The numbers refer to the lines in the Third Bagre.

musical instruments, xylophones or drums, to play (or be played) throughout the performances. The other major actors are the guides, who are first graders assigned to each neophyte to show them what to do and what not to do. They have a special responsibility for seeing that the neophytes obey the many prohibitions, on food and of other kinds, that are placed upon them but from which they are gradually released. The guides may be male or female depending upon the sex of their charges.

BAGRE RECITATIONS

In the First Bagre, there were two recitations, the White and the Black. The White was recited to the first graders (the White Bagre members) and consisted largely of an account of the sequence of ceremonies themselves as well as the way that human woes led up to the present performances. The version of the Black was more cosmological as well as being more philosophical than subsequent ones; it recounted the visit of one of the two original men to Heaven where he greeted God and was shown the creation of a child. He was also taught much about how human beings came to learn about the world in which they now operate, but through the intermediaries of the beings of the wild rather than by God himself. Indeed, a major theme is the struggle between the two, as well as the struggle between the 'father' and the 'mother' about the ownership of the child ('God's child'). The Second Bagre, published in 1981, has a White Bagre which is substantially shorter than the First (3,940 lines as compared with 6,133), but the Black is slightly longer (5,764 lines as against 5,515). Both place little stress on either God or the beings of the wild. Humans invent their own culture.

Finally, in 1979, two versions of the Black Bagre (The Third Bagre) were recorded in Biro and in Gomble, outlying parts of Birifu, where the reciter was the same in both cases, being the Headman of Biro. Hence the versions are similar in many ways, though the latter is 2,781 lines in length, compared with 1,646 in the former. Both versions start with an invocation, in which they greet the Bagre god (*nminti*) and then the 'people of the room' including those of their forefathers who have recited the Bagre in the past, leaving behind only the 'children' who fumble with it and 'cannot know all' as their predecessors had done. Such oral recitations emphasize the perpetual debt and sense of inferiority one has to the ancestors, since unlike in a written culture their words cannot be recorded for posterity, but only imperfectly remembered and recited publicly, without the possibility of confirmation or correction.

Turning to the content, in Gomble the 'people of the room', the assembled participants, once the god 'has told' of his coming, climb up to the roof top where they will see the stars. There then follows the mention of a number of stars and constellations, the Star of God, the axe of God, the stones of the chief's granary (or the granary of a rich man), the cock and his chicks; these are matters of the heavens. The Biro Bagre begins in a similar way, with different forefathers, but with the star of God, the ox, the cock, but the head blacksmith replaces the stones of the chief's granary. In no other context do I know the LoDagaa developing a star-lore, an explicit knowledge of the heavens, nor did my colleague Kum Gandah. The night sky is always there and the constellations may always suggest the shape of objects to individual observers, suggestions which may at times resemble one another. Such an account of the heavens is an ever-present possibility even when star-lore is not 'institutionalized' in a more formal ('cultural') manner.[25]

The account of man's beginning opens up further such possibilities. As distinct from the First (Birifu) Bagre, which I published in 1972, there are already people living on earth even before the 'creation' story begins – old men and little children living together in a house. There are also animals, the dulu bird who acts like the first men in the 1972 version by going to consult a diviner (about food); the diviner is a lizard whom the dulu later eats. He also needs protection against the rain. The (male) rain comes and fertilizes the (female) earth, as in other versions. Then we shift suddenly to the male and the female (humans) who are being rained on and who want shelter. The other versions too are concerned with people's initial helplessness in face of the world, not knowing how to provide themselves with shelter or with food. The First Bagre (1972) I have described as theocentric

---

[25] 'We have no assurance', writes Stith Thompson about the astral interpretations of mythologies, 'nor does it even seem likely, that most primitive peoples really concerned themselves with the heavenly bodies' (1951: 394). While that is hardly true of the sun and moon, there is certainly great variation in knowledge of the stars.

because all these benefits come ultimately from God, but they do so, except for the initial act of procreation, through the intermediaries of the beings of the wild ('the fairies') who not only show humans how things should be done ('God's path') but try to lead them astray in order for them to follow their own. It is the core of their struggle that dominates much of the first version of the Bagre, together with the problems of parenthood and the performance of the Bagre itself.

In later versions (e.g. the Second Bagre) I argue that it is much more a question of 'humans make themselves' even though God provides them with some of his tools.[26] In Gomble and Biro we find another variant of the creation theme, perhaps more unexpected in view of all that has been written, including by myself, on the nature of the High God who retires from the world after the initial act of creation. Here he plays a more active part.

The relationship between God (*na-angmin* – chief god) and god (*ngmin*) is not at all clear in the First Bagre. I then tried to distinguish between the two by capitalizing God in the first case. But the myth speaks of god's breeze at a certain point (line 1,409) and of God's breeze at another (line 1,006). Both are possible. The god (*ngmin*) who descends (line 1,991) to the Bagre ceremony I have translated as God, which was certainly against my principle of translation. It is elsewhere said to be the Bagre god (*ngmin*) who descends, for God himself we don't know where he is. But the Bagre god (one can never say Bagre Na-angmin, Bagre God) is certainly a refraction of God himself and may at times be identified with him.

The place I have most obviously gone against my principles of translation was in the final passages of the White Bagre where the neophytes are asking the question:

> The beings of the wild
> and God,
> which of them brought Bagre? (lines 6,005–7)

God here should be 'god' (*ngmin*) but the recitation goes on:

> they replied, 'well,
> God created them,

[26] Goody 1998.

put them on earth,
and they sat there empty-handed' (lines 6,008–11)

While *ngmin* is again used here, in LoDagaa belief it is God
(*na-angmin*) who created us, even if he left us empty-handed. It was
then that the ancestors found out what we needed to do. Elsewhere it
is explained that they were helped by the beings of the wild. God (here
ngmin) knows all about us but does not come down to earth because
humankind would trouble him too much about their problems (line
6,059). So he sent another person 'who is more powerful than us all'
(line 6,084). That person is the Bagre god (*Bo ngmin* or *wen*), who is
the god who descends and intervenes in the performances.

The difference between God and god is explained in response to a
neophyte's question:

The one
we follow
in this matter,
is it God (*na-angmin*) we follow
or is it a god (*ngmin*)? (lines 5,244–8)

To this the elder replies:

'Well,
we follow
God.
He is the senior
but we can't see him.
It is god who comes down to people.
That is what we call god' (lines 5,251–7)

The difference is that

'A god is here
and God is there' (lines 5,241–2):

god is the one who is 'visible', who descends, and who is a refraction
of God. That is why at times god is used for God (as the Creator)
and why, in response to my colleague's prompting, I have sometimes translated *ngmin* by God, when I thought the usage reflected
LoDagaa thought. That is a dangerous procedure, but I did so only

when my own interpretation and that of my collaborator, Kum Gandah, coincided. 'God's child', whom we follow, is Napolo, whom he created.

In the Biro and Gomble versions God intervenes directly and continues to do so. The rain came and the first man and woman feel cold.

> They shivered with cold
> and called on God.
> When they had done so,
> God it was
> who came down quickly,
> took a small hoe
> and some axes,
> gave them to the man
> and he went to the bush.[27]

God himself provided the man with his instruments, not the beings of the wild, as in the First Bagre, nor was it left to the man himself as in the Second. After that initial intervention the man took over the work of building a house with the help of 'the clever young girl' who was the 'woman', his wife. She mixed the swish and the man called his 'brothers' to come along to help him, just as he would today, leaving aside the question of their origin (or of his). The house being built, God 'performed his works'. The man went off to sleep and had an erection, so he called the woman. But she told him he had to come over to her. There was a quarrel but after all the 'clever young girl' came over and pulled out his penis and satisfied herself. The 'foolish man' then repeated the act. In the morning

> … God, it was he
> with all his wonders,
> came down suddenly
> and went and asked the woman.[28]

She told him what had happened and they were 'ashamed' at 'spoiling' one another but later got on with the matter of bringing forth a child. Why the shame?

---

[27] Goody and Gandah 2002: 218–26.   [28] Goody and Gandah 2002: 456–9.

It relates to the central prohibitions of the Bagre. These are of several major kinds. There are the food taboos which are placed on the neophytes at the Announcement and gradually lifted during the performances, beginning with that on the shea nut. It is because the fruit bat saves us from breaking this taboo, by showing us when it is ripe, that it is among our Bagre 'things'; this discovery begins the Bagre. He refuses to share the fruit with his wife as she had refused to sleep with him the previous night. Other foods too are forbidden, then allowed to the neophytes in the course of the ceremonies, some of which are even named after the food itself (e.g. the Bagre of Beans). But the major emphasis insisted on throughout is the taboo on fighting and on sexual intercourse. Both have to be avoided during its course. The first prohibition (on quarrelling) occurs widely in several situations where people meet together, for example, in markets, where it is a particular example of the widespread institution of 'the peace of the market'. Again fighting, leading to the shedding of blood, is forbidden between members of the parish that hold allegiance to the same Earth shrine. But fighting (quarrelling) is not universally frowned upon. One should fight in a just cause, for example, to defend oneself or a kinsman.

This conflicting valuation is even clearer with sexual intercourse. There is not the same obvious reason for banning one of the great pleasures of humans and animals, though it is true that it may give rise to conflict and even to feud and war, 'women' being seen as one of the causes, by men. But even legitimate sex, between man and wife, runs against the principles of Bagre where each neophyte is individually selected and individually processed. True, he or she is backed and helped by kinsfolk. But in some significant ways, the Bagre overrides the demands of kinship. For example, seniority in Bagre is not determined by birth but by the date of initiation (as is often the case in associations of this general kind). So the cross-cutting intimacy of sex is forbidden to the Bagre neophytes in a very severe manner. And at performance time at least it is forbidden both by god and by God. But the ambivalence has wider repercussions because, as in the biblical story, there seem to be some qualms built into the act itself, perhaps because it is so excluding.

Returning to the recitations, the central recording of the Lawra Bagre differs from all others partly because of its content, which I have described, and partly because of its form. The content includes minimal versions of the White and Black as we have come across them elsewhere, but we do find both verse and prose versions of the Coming of the Kusiele, a clan legend that is essentially about the doings of the ancestor who found the clan's present lands and who inaugurated the Bagre there. But he has no explicit help from God, from god or from the beings of the wild. He himself does what he has to do.

As far as form is concerned, the recording of the Lawra Bagre differs from all the others we have made, in its very nature. In earlier cases we only recorded the recitation which is recognized by the actors as a special form of speech (what I have elsewhere called 'standard oral forms'). But here we allowed the recorder to continue to run during the rest of the ceremony when the senior members, the leading members in particular, were trying to organize the shape of what had to be done – and to agree upon the course of events. Such material provides an idea of the course of these proceedings, of the role of the leading members and the nature of their autonomy, of the degree of uncertainty that exists and of the role of consultation. It emphasizes how different the nature of such a ritual is from, say, the Christian Mass, or from a Buddhist ceremony in Taiwan, where everything proceeds according to the formula written down in a book which the priest constantly consults.[29] Here there is no written template, only the attempt to reconstruct a long and complex performance, with its accompanying recitation, from the recitations of the leading participants. This recording offers an example of how that is done, which is very far from the outsider's notion of automatic and stable custom dominating the social scene. Like the Bagre material, more generally, it should make us reconsider those ideas of 'traditional' society and of 'primitive' mentality.

[29] Goody 1986.

CHAPTER 8

From oral to written: an anthropological breakthrough in storytelling

Oral forms of recitation are held to give primacy to the narrative. My own experience is that, as I have argued in Chapter 5, narrative folktales are mainly for children and that adults do not privilege the fictional narrative, which is often held to be untruth and hence subject to criticism, as in the Puritanical Complex. As we have seen, the emergence of 'visible language', of writing, made an important contribution to new forms of literature, such as the novel. But more than that it had a profound influence on society at large and specifically on the speed of social change in the accumulation of knowledge.

The telling of tales is often thought to be characteristic of all human discourse and it is fashionable to speak of narrative as a universal form of expression, one which is applicable both to the life experiences of individuals and to the dramas of social interaction. Storytelling in oral cultures is seen as the foundation on which the novel is built and the activity is regarded as the focus of much creativity in literate societies. Blind Homer was the model, putting all his oral imagination into the epic. In discussing storytelling we are clearly leading into the topics of fiction and the novel. But not all storytelling is fictional; it can also involve personal narratives, however, although typically the activity is associated with oral cultures, with 'the singer (or teller) of tales'.[1] In his article on the subject, Walter Benjamin sees the storyteller as disappearing with the arrival of the novel, whose dissemination he associates with the coming of printing, and the telling of tales is no longer directly linked with direct experience of human interaction in the same way as before.[2]

[1] Lord 1960.   [2] Benjamin 1968a: 87.

The timing of the appearance of the novel is subject to discussion. Mikhail Bakhtin uses the term (or 'novelness') in a much more extended sense. But in dealing with origins more concretely, he traces the novel (of 'adventure time') back to the Greek romances of the second century CE, to the novel of everyday time in the story of *The Golden Ass* of Apuleius; there is a third 'chronotope' centred on biographical time, but this does not produce any novels at this period. All three forms are harbingers of the modern novel.[3] That is basically a product of the advent of printing in the late fifteenth century, but as we see from these early examples, the nature of storytelling had already radically changed with the coming of writing. Indeed, I want to argue that, contrary to much received opinion, narrative (already in 1566 used for 'an account, narration, a tale, recital') is not so much a universal feature of the human situation as one that is promoted by literacy and subsequently by printing.

Today the word narrative has come to have an iconic, indeed a cant, significance in western literary and social science circles. I suggest a rather different approach, using the term narrative in a much tighter way, implying a plot with a firm sequential structure, marked by a beginning, a middle and an end in the Aristotelian manner. Otherwise one is involved in a similar kind of extension to that which Derrida has tried to give to 'writing' in which term he includes all 'traces', including memory traces. That usage makes it impossible to make the at-times essential distinction between written archives and memory banks. The same is true for the use of the term 'literature' for oral genres, what I call 'standard oral forms', since this usage, which I have used in Chapter 3, obscures important analytical differences. Likewise narrative is sometimes held to include any vaguely sequential discourse. 'What is the narrative?' is the often-heard cry. When I employ the term, I do so in an altogether tighter sense, as a standard form that has a definite plot that proceeds by structured stages.

Let me take a recent, authoritative example of the wider usage. In his book on *The Political Unconscious*,[4] which is subtitled 'Narrative as a Socially Symbolic Act', the literary critic Fredric Jameson sees his task as attempting to 'restructure the problematics of ideology, of

---

[3] Clark and Holquist 1984. Doody 1996 rejects the categorical distinction, found only in English, between romance and the novel, placing the origin of the latter in ancient Greece.
[4] Jameson 1981.

the unconscious and of desire, of representation, of history, and of cultural production, around the all-informing process of narrative, which I take to be … the central function or instance of the human mind'.⁵ There is little one can say about such a terrifyingly inclusive aim centred upon such an all-embracing concept of the process of narrative. He is not alone in this usage. Some psychologists view storytelling as a prime mode of cognition; at a recent conference on the subject, philosophers proposed the creation of narrative as one of the key competencies of humankind. In attempting to query this and similar assumptions, I want also to tackle another. In an article on 'the narrative structure of reality', reflecting a further all-inclusive use of this term, Stuart Hall remarked, 'we make an absolutely too simple and false distinction between narratives about the real and the narratives of fiction, that is, between news and adventure stories'.⁶ Is that really 'too simple and false'? In my experience the distinction exists if not universally at least transculturally. Indeed, I would go further and suggest it is an intrinsic feature of linguistic discourse. How do we know someone is not deceiving us, telling us a fiction, a story, a tale, if we make no such distinction?

As Orwell remarked about Catalonia in his 'Looking back on the Spanish War', 'This kind of thing is frightening to me, because it often gives me the feeling that the very concept of objective truth is fading out of the world. After all, the chances are that those lies or at any rate similar lies will pass into history.'⁷ Whether what we are being told is a fiction or a deliberate lie (implying intentionality), both are departures from the literal truth. It does not matter to me in this context whether there is philosophical justification for objective truth, with a correspondence theory of truth. I need only an acknowledgement of the fact that the actors need to distinguish between truth and untruth. It is true that psychology, psychoanalysis and perhaps sociology too, have qualified our view of the lie from the standpoint of the individual, in an attempt to elicit the reasons why people do not always tell the truth. But in dyadic interaction, in social communication between two or more persons, the question of the truth or untruth of a statement remains critical. Did he or did

⁵ Jameson 1981: 13.
⁶ *Southern Review*, Adelaide, 17 (1984): 3–17, quoted in Sommerville 1996: 173.
⁷ Orwell 1968.

he not post the letter I gave him as he claimed? Untruth may not be a lie. It may also involve fantasy or fiction, fantasy being the latter's non-realistic equivalent. Fantasy does not invite a literal comparison with a truthful account of events at the surface level. But fiction may do just that, may make a claim to truth value. That was the difference between romances and novels in England at the beginning of the eighteenth century. The realistic novels of Defoe and others deliberately invite an assessment of the truth or otherwise of the tale. The writers often claim truth for fiction, not the underlying experiential truth but literal, factual truth.

The distinction runs parallel to that commonly made between history and myth, marked respectively by linear and circular time; the former in effect requires the availability of documents and hence of writing, but its absence does not exclude a sense of the past in oral cultures, of which myth is one variety, only of 'history' in the formal meaning of a study based upon the examination of documents. We might wish to qualify this distinction for our own purposes but there can be little doubt that it emerged within the actor's frame-of-reference; the Homeric *mythos* was set apart from *historia* and even *logos*, both of which implied some assessment of truth.[8]

In the absence of writing, communication in oral cultures has to rely largely on speech. Yet experience in Africa suggests that such discourse rather rarely consisted in the telling of tales, if by that we mean personal and fictional stories created for adults. The LoDagaa of northern Ghana certainly make a distinction of this kind between what I translate as 'proper speech' (*yil miong*) and lies (*ziiri*), between truth and falsehood. 'Proper speech' would include what I have translated as 'The Myth of the Bagre', but that recitation itself raises the question of whether what it offers is a lie or whether it is 'God's way', God's truth. Folktales are not referred to as lies since they make no claim to the truth but neither are they truth (for example, animals speak and behave like humans; people do not 'believe' they are really like this, or that the moon is made of blue cheese); as I shall claim, such tales are largely addressed to children and they do verge upon the lie in the Platonic sense, as we see from the account of a LoDagaa writer.

[8] Goody and Walt 1963: 321ff.

For the problem with fictional narrative emerges from another angle in a rather imaginative biography by a member of this same LoDagaa group, Malidoma Somé, who claims his people make no distinction between the natural and supernatural or between reality and the imagined (which I doubt). Somé is described in his book, *Of Water and the Spirit*, as 'a medicine man and diviner' as well as holding a PhD from Brandeis and giving lectures at a spiritual centre in America. He decided to test the absence of these distinctions by showing the elders of his African village a video recording of *Star Trek*. They interpreted the film as portraying 'the current affairs in the day-to-day lives of some other people living in the world'. 'I could not make them understand', he writes, 'that all this was not real.' 'Even though stories abound in my culture, we have no word for fiction. The only way I could get across to them the Western concept of fiction was to associate fiction with telling lies.'[9] That assertion corresponds with my own experience, at least as far as adults are concerned.

Truthful narratives among the LoDagaa, in my own experience, would be those relating to one's own personal life, perhaps accounts of labour migration to the gold mines in the south of the country; or those of local feuds or wars that happened before the coming of the colonial conquerors early last century. Stories of this kind are occasionally told but their place is rather marginal; narrative and storytelling, even non-fictional, are hardly as central as is visualized by those seeking to reconstruct the forms of discourse in early literate culture and supposedly inherited from yet earlier purely oral ones.

The discussions of Derrida, Hall and Jameson seem to me to represent the elimination or neglect of historically and analytically useful distinctions in a misguided, post-modern-influenced drive against 'binarism' and towards holism. In fact the distinctions we have adopted do not threaten the overall unity of the *esprit humain*, the human mind, nor do they embody a we/they view of the world.

Turning more specifically to the question of narrative in oral cultures, there are five aspects of 'literary' forms I want to look at; these are legends, epics, myths, folktales and finally personal narratives. The epic is a distinctly narrative genre, partly fictional,

---

[9] Somé 1994: 8–9.

though often having a basis in heroic deeds on the field of bat-
tle. It is defined as a kind of narrative poetry which celebrates the
achievements of some heroic personage of history or of tradition
(that is, which may have a quota of fact). The great scholar of early
literature, Chadwick, saw the epic as the typical product of what he
called the Heroic Age, peopled by chiefs, warriors and tribesmen.[10]
Since this genre is usually regarded as emerging in pre-literate
societies, much academic research has been directed at trying to
show that, for example, the Homeric poems, as epics, were composed in pre-literate rather than literate cultures. During the 1930s
the Harvard classical scholars Parry[11] and Lord[12] made a series of
recordings of songs in Yugoslav cafés and aimed to show that their
style, especially in the use of formulaic expressions, made them
representative of epics of the oral tradition. However, Yugoslavia
was by no means a purely oral culture and its verbal forms were
strongly influenced by the presence of writing, and especially of
written religions. Some of the recitations actually appeared as texts
in song books which were available to the 'singers of tales' and there
was reference back and forth. It is also the case more generally that
the societies of the 'Heroic Age' where the epic flourished were
ones where early literacy was present. By contrast, in the purely oral
cultures of Africa, the epic is a rarity, except on the southern fringes
of the Sahara, which have been much influenced by Islam and by
its literary forms.

Africa south of the Sahara was, until recently, one of the main
areas of the world where writing was totally absent; that was also
the case in recent times with parts of South America (together with
Australasia and the Pacific). Most of South America was transformed
by the Spanish and Portuguese in the sixteenth century, though a
few remote areas escaped their overwhelming, hegemonic influence.
Africa offers the most straightforward case of the purely oral society, even though influenced by the written civilizations of Europe in
the west, of the Mediterranean in the north and of the Arabs in the
east. It is also a continent whose oral literature has received much
attention. The main work of synthesis has been carried out by Ruth
Finnegan. On the epic she is very definite:

---

[10] Chadwick 1932–40.   [11] Parry 1971.   [12] Lord 1960.

Epic is often assumed to be the typical poetic form of non-literate peoples ... Surprisingly, however, this does not seem to be borne out by the African evidence. At least in the more obvious sense of a 'relatively long narrative poem', epic hardly seems to occur in sub-Saharan Africa apart from forms like the [written] Swahili utenzi which are directly attributable to Arabic literary influence.[13]

What has been called epic in Africa is often prose rather than poetry, though some of the lengthy praise poems of South Africa have something of an epic quality about them. Otherwise most frequently mentioned are the Mongo-Nkundo tales from the Congo; these too are mainly prose and resemble other African examples in their general features. The most famous is the Lianja epic running to 120 pages of print for text and translation. It covers the birth and tribulations of the hero, his travels, the leadership of his people and finally his death. Finnegan suggests that the original form might have been 'a very loosely related bundle of separate episodes, told on separate occasions and not necessarily thought of as one single work of art (though recent and sophisticated narrators say that ideally it should be told at one sitting)'.[14] In other words a similar type of amalgamation of short tales may have taken place under the impact of writing as apparently occurred with the Gilgamesh epic of Mesopotamia.

Of course, much has been collected since Finnegan was writing, specifically in connection with 'history', but that collection has not been very disciplined in terms of anthropological verification of sources, context and audience, and the cultures themselves have been so influenced by literacy and by schools that it is difficult to see African society as 'purely oral' in the way assumed. Most recitations belong to what I call the 'lecto-oral' and have been influenced by the presence of writing and a hegemonic religion, just as Finnegan viewed the presence of the epic in sub-Saharan Africa. The presence of schools, of a national (literate) state, of written religions, of the strong pressure to invent the past has influenced previously purely oral forms.

We do find some poetry of a legendary kind in the *mvet* literature of the Fang peoples of Gabon and Cameroon, as well as in the recitations of the griots among the Mande south of the Sahara.

---

[13] Finnegan 1970: 108.   [14] Finnegan 1970: 109.

Finnegan concludes: 'In general terms and apart from Islamic influences, epic seems to be of remarkably little significance in African oral literature, and the a priori assumption that epic is the natural form for many non-literate peoples turns out here to have little support'.[15]

Since Finnegan's earlier book, the picture with regard to longer compositions has somewhat changed, both in respect of 'mythical' and of 'legendary' (including epic) material. As far as longer 'myths' are concerned, we now have three published volumes of the Bagre of the LoDagaa, the first version consisting of some 12,000 short lines in length, and taking some eight hours to recite. This work is concerned not with the deeds of heroes (as in epics) but with the creation of man's world, with the position of humans in relation to their God and their gods, with problems of philosophy and of life.

It contrasts sharply with the recitation of the griots of Bambara and Mali, whose products may well have been influenced by Islamic literature. The griots (the word is in general use) are a type of minstrel belonging to an endogamous caste-like group. They perform mainly at the courts of chiefs but also on other secular, public occasions, for the societies in which they are found are kingdoms, unlike the acephalous, tribal LoDagaa where praise singing is little developed and legends are no more than migration histories of the clan or lineage.[16]

Listen on the other hand to the account of his profession given by the griot Tinguidji, who was recorded by Seydou.

We, the mâbos, only beg from nobles; there where a noble is, I am there. A mâbo doesn't bother except where there is some value. If he sees a poor man and begs from him, if he sees him with nothing and praises him, if he sees someone who has the air and praises him, a mâbo who acts like that is worth nothing. As for me, if someone is not my superior, I don't praise him; I give to him freely. That is how I am, me, Tinguidji.

(Nous, le mâbos, nous ne quémandons, qu'auprès des nobles: là où il y a un noble, j'y suis aussi. Un mâbo ne se préoccupe pas de ce qui n'a pas de valeur: s'il voit un pauvre et qu'il quémande auprès de lui, s'il le voit dénué de tout et qu'il le loue, s'il en voit un qui en a l'air et qu'il le loue, un mâbo qui agit de la sorte, ne vaut rien. Moi, celui qui ne m'est pas superieur, je ne le loue pas. Celui qui n'est pas plus que moi, je ne le loue pas; je lui donne. Voilà comment je suis, moi, Tinguidji.)[17]

---

[15] Finnegan 1970: 110.   [16] Goody 1977a.   [17] Seydou 1972: 13–14.

It would therefore be wrong to assume that all the activities of the griots were directed towards pleasing or praising the aristocracy in return for largesse. There were some who adopted an aggressive attitude towards the world in general, 'vulgar and unscrupulous griots whose only aim is to extort gifts and favours and who, to that end, work with so much unselfconsciousness and audacity, praise, and insult him using the dithyrambic panegyric and the vindictive diatribe, in both the language of the nobility and the most terrible slang'.[18] Apart from these differences of approach, griots differed in other ways but all belonged to the 'gens castés', the *nyeenybe*, the caste-like artisans which included smiths, wood-carvers, leather-workers, weavers (who are also singers, the *mâbo*); these minstrels, 'artisans of the word and of the musical arts', included the 'intellectual-griots who have studied the Quran, the *awlube* or drummers, who are attached to a particular family whose history, genealogy and praises they sing, the *jeeli* of Mandingo origin, who play many instruments, are unattached and make their living by their profession, and *nyemakala*, wandering singers and guitarists who organize evening entertainments'.[19]

The intellectual-griots were those who studied the Quran, giving support to Finnegan's point about Islamic influences. The bulk of the epics in Africa are found on the fringes of the Sahara, where such influences are strong and of long duration. The Fulani epic of Silâmaka and Poullôri recounts the story of a chief's son and his slave, together with a companion, who attempt to relieve their country of its debt of tribute. It is an epic of chiefship recited within a culture that was linked to the written tradition of Islam; A.-H. Bâ has described the society of that time as village-based, with each village headed by a man who was literate in Arabic,[20] but in any case the language and its literature were known throughout the towns of the region, influencing the nature of local life and thought, especially its artistic forms as well as its history.[21]

Under these conditions, narrative recitations of an epic kind appear. The model is provided by Islamic tradition; they are found in complex chiefdoms, the rulers of which are served by professionals

---

[18] Seydou 1972: 15.   [19] Seydou 1972: 17–20.   [20] Seydou 1972: 81.
[21] Hiskett 1957; Wilks 1963; Hodgkin 1966.

of various kinds, including praise singers. Being focussed upon the past deeds of the chiefly ancestors (the history of the state), such songs take upon themselves a narrative format, recounting struggles of heroes of earlier times.

It should be pointed out that the content of this Fulani epic was 'fixed' in certain broad features, but varied enormously in its telling. Seydou describes how the legend crossed frontiers, was spread by the mouths of griots who, 'each in his own fashion and according to his own practice, have enriched, transformed, rebuilt from diverse elements borrowed from other recitals'. So the epic ended up as a recitation which some have seen as part of a complete cycle, whether in the Bambara literature or among the people, that is, in Fulani.[22] As a result we find a great number and variety of versions,[23] which develop one particular episode and exalt this or that hero, because it is recited for both the contending parties in the struggle, the Fulani and the Bambara. Each time the griots are playing to a specific but varying audience. They live by the responses of that audience; they travel, play the lute, and change their story to fit the community in which they are working. In other words, while the Fulani epic, like the epic in general, seems to occur in a society influenced by writing, the form it takes varies considerably depending upon the bard, the time, the situation. Such variants should not, to my mind, be regarded as part of a definitive cycle, for that exists only when inventiveness has stopped and the epic has been circumscribed in text, but rather as part of an expanding universe around a narrative theme.

Both Finnegan (1970) and Tedlock (1983) reject the proposition that the epic is characteristically a feature of purely oral cultures and associate it with the early literate cultures of the Old World. Finnegan works mainly on Africa, Tedlock on the Americas. The latter concludes that the only 'epic texts with long metrical runs come from folk traditions within larger literate cultures'.[24] However, in commenting upon these conclusions, Rumsey claims that recitations found among a group of neighbouring societies in the New Guinea Highlands do constitute 'an oral epic tradition'. The examples he

[22] Seydou 1972: 9–10.
[23] For example, Veillard 1931; Bâ and Kesteloot 1969.
[24] Tedlock 1983: 8.

gives have a strong narrative content and are marked by formulaic repetition of the kind to which Parry and Lord draw attention in their analysis of Yugoslav songs. He discusses two kinds of story, *kange* and *temari*, which have been assimilated to the European distinction between 'fiction' and 'factual',[25] but which others have seen as having more to do with the distinction between the world of narrated events and the here-now world from which they are being narrated.[26] Nevertheless, some kind of 'truth value' does seem to be involved. *Kange* tend to be told indoors, at night, after the evening meal; with a single individual holding the floor for ten to twenty minutes, there is a turn-taking rule with a 'ratified speaker'. Some stories are told by women but to children rather than to the world at large.

Rumsey compares these tales to European epics. But while they are certainly narrative and many have a central 'heroic' character, they are short recitations, mostly running between three hundred and seven hundred lines in length. It is no part of my intent to deny the presence of fictional narrative in oral cultures, merely to say that long narratives are rare and any narrative at all less frequent than has often been thought, because, I would suggest, of the inherent problems of fiction. The fact that Rumsey finds (short) epics in the New Guinea Highlands and that Finnegan denies them for Black Africa and Tedlock for the Americas in itself raises a problem of presence and absence. Why should such a problem exist at all? Why are epics, defined by Tedlock as 'a heroic narrative with a metrical, sung text',[27] relatively rare in oral cultures? Why do narratives, especially fictional ones, not dominate the discourse of oral cultures, especially in artistic genres, in the way that much contemporary theory about storytelling requires? We are referring here not only to long, substantial recitations. The so-called epics from the New Guinea Highlands are quite short. Even if we were to see these tales as epics (and they are certainly narrative), we have a problem of what this implies that needs to be faced beyond saying that this distribution is 'cultural'. That is a question to which we will return later.

What about other forms of narrative, of storytelling? Legends are often linked to epics, but do not take the same metrical form. Despite their presumed association with the written word (*legenda*,

---

[25] Rumsey 2006. [26] Merlan 1995. [27] Tedlock 1983: 8.

what is read) in their association with written saints tales and the like, they are found in oral cultures, in tribal ones in the form of clan histories, in chiefdoms in the form of dynastic ones. In the latter case they are often much more fragmentary than is thought; in some cases the state histories just take the form of drum titles for chiefs and of chronicles rather than narratives in a stronger sense.

Once again myths, which are perhaps the most studied genre, are too often assumed to be universal. Mythologies are (in the sense of universal constructions of a supernatural order) but myths in the sense of long, supernaturally oriented, recitations; of the type recorded for the Zuni of North America or the Bagre of the LoDagaa, which take hours to recite, these are very unevenly distributed and much less narrative in form, however, than the early Hindu Mahabharata or even the Gilgamesh 'epic' of Mesopotamia (both creations of literate cultures) would lead us to suppose. Myths are standard oral forms; mythologies are bodies of tales about the supernatural derived from a multiplicity of sources and reconstructed by the observer, as in the case of the *Mythologiques* of Lévi-Strauss.[28]

Myth does a number of different things. It has some narrative element. But the importance of that has been greatly exaggerated by the collectors of myths (and mythologies) who have often deliberately asked their respondents for stories and not cared much about the philosophical, theological, wisdom aspects of the recitation. That is an error that has led in the past, before the portable audio recorder, to considerable misconceptions. At one level I would liken the Bagre to the Bible in the number of tasks it performs. There is the etiological narrative in Genesis, the 'wisdom' of Proverbs, the ritual prescriptions of Leviticus. What there is not is a sequential narrative or even continuity running throughout. Hartman[29] writes not only of the Bible's uniqueness but of its unity. Every piece of writing is at some level unique but that is not I think what is being said. In any case, unity is not its obvious characteristic; books have been aggregated together as a canon almost haphazardly. The unity is given by the ritual context, not by the text.

What I have called 'The Myth of the Bagre' found among the LoDagaa of northern Ghana will serve as an example. It concerns

[28] Lévi-Strauss 1969.   [29] Hartman 1999.

serious supernatural affairs, coming into the category of 'proper speech', and is associated with membership of the Bagre society, which is held to confer medical (and in a sense spiritual) benefits. This long recitation takes six to eight hours to recite in the accepted fashion, with each phrase (or 'line' in my transcription) being repeated by the audience of neophytes and members (their guides), and then the whole process is repeated twice yet again by other Speakers. The time taken varies with the Speaker and the degree of elaboration he employs, as well as with the point in the ceremony at which the recitation takes place.

It consists of two parts, the White and the Black. The first is an account of the different ceremonies which are held over several weeks, and is recited up to the point in the sequence that has been reached. The Black, on the other hand, is intended only for the ears of those men (women are now excluded) who have passed through the first initiation and includes some account of how humans were created (and how they learnt to create themselves) as well as how they came to acquire the basic elements of their culture, that is farming, hunting, the raising of livestock, the making of iron, the brewing of beer.

This is 'proper speech' because it concerns humankind's relationship with the supernatural, especially with the beings of the wild who act as intermediaries, sometimes mischievous, between humans and God. And while the outsider may look upon the recitation as 'myth', as an imaginative expression of humankind's relationship with the world and with the divine, for the LoDagaa it is real enough (as the Bible is for many of us), even though the possibility that it is not always true is often raised. Indeed the salvation against trouble, including death itself, that the Bagre medicine offers to new initiates is subsequently shown in the Black Bagre to be an illusion; hopes are raised, only later to be crushed.

However, the point that I want to make here is that, leaving aside the question of fiction, of truth or falsehood, the narrative content of the recitation is limited. A certain framework is provided for the White Bagre, the account of the ceremonies, which explains how the Bagre was started after consultation with a diviner following a series of troubles adjudged to have transcendental origins. There is obviously a sequence in the account of the ceremonies and of their associated prohibitions and injunctions. But this hardly takes a narrative form. What we do find, on three or four occasions, is short narratives, resembling folktales, embedded in the recitation at certain points in the context of a particular ceremony. Page has remarked upon similar modules embedded in the Homeric poems.[30] These tales do assume a definitive narrative form, with a beginning, middle and an end. They also seem to require a different commitment regarding 'belief' than the bulk of the recitation. They are obviously tales.

The Black Bagre begins in a more promising manner as far as narrative is concerned. The elder of two 'brothers' experiences troubles which he attributes to mystical causes. He consults a diviner to find out which. As a result he sets out on a long and arduous journey, a quest, which takes him to the Other World. Coming across a river, probably that separating this world from the other, he meets an old man, probably the High God. With the aid of the spider, he climbs up to Heaven (to 'God's country'). There he meets 'a slender young girl' and the High God shows them how a child is created in a mystical way. The recitation continues at length with the man and woman quarrelling about the ownership of the male child and his education. Meanwhile they are introduced, with the aid of the beings of the wild ('fairies'), to various aspects of LoDagaa culture, to the making of iron, the cultivation of crops, the brewing of beer, and eventually to the procreation, rather than the creation, of children. While a loose narrative frame exists, the greater part of the recitation concerns the description of central aspects of culture, especially its technological processes. And much of the rest deals with philosophical problems (like the problem of evil) and theological ones (like the relationship between the High God and the beings of the wild). Narrativity is not the dominant characteristic. And even so, these long recitations, myths, are very unevenly distributed in cultures. The LoDagaa have them; none of their neighbours apparently do (except some of the Bagre).

What does seem to be universal, at least in the Old World, are folktales. We find these everywhere, often in a surprisingly similar form – short tales, sometimes followed by an inconsequential tail or end, involving as actors humans, animals and often gods. We may

[30] Page 1973.

think of the Ananse stories of the Akan (with the Spider as trickster) as prototypical, together with their Caribbean variants, the Nancy tales of Brer Rabbit.

Those tales have been taken by some observers as representative of 'primitive thought'. Frequently they are envisaged as being told around the evening fire to a mixed audience. My own experience in West Africa is rather different. As I have often mentioned, such stories, like those in the works of the brothers Grimm, are mainly aimed at children and do not represent the thought of adults in oral cultures, although they may also listen. By far the greater part are short folktales ('fairy tales') of the kind told to children, not the fare of ordinary adult consumption. They represent 'primitive mentality' only to the extent that 'Jack and the Beanstalk' in Europe today can be held to represent 'contemporary modernity'. They are set aside as children's discourse. Indeed, fiction generally is for the young; adults demand more serious matter, not fictional 'stories' of life or even of the Other World, but truthful or near-truthful accounts. The possibility that these tales are the main forms of narrative fiction in many oral cultures carries another implication, that fiction itself is seen as appropriate for children but not perhaps for adults.

Finally, we come to personal narratives. In psychoanalysis the 'talking cure' requires both analyst and analysand to construct 'a case history' out of fragmentary conversations, 'histories' that appear in the form of Freud's Dora and the Wolfman. The case history is never produced autonomously but is elicited and created; and it is a creation of a literate society and of literate procedures; like the Mesopotamian Gilgamesh or the contemporary Mungo epic in all probability, it represents a piecing together of fragments to form a continuous narrative, which is never (or very rarely) given to the enquirer on a plate, except in writing.

It seems natural that we should create a narrative summary of our lives, for incorporation in a CV, for presenting to an analyst, for elaboration in a diary or an autobiography. But how far are such narratives called for in purely oral cultures? I can think of few if any situations where this happens. It is I, the anthropologist, the psychologist, the historian, who tries to construct life histories (like other histories) from the fragments of knowledge that have come my way, or from the arduous struggle of asking questions and getting one's respondent to respond, to articulate for me what no other situation would prompt him or her to do. Life histories do not emerge automatically; they are heavily constructed. The constructed nature of case histories is superbly brought out by Gilbert Lewis in his *A Failure of Treatment*.[31] The history does not exactly traduce the 'facts', but it gives a narrative shape to the fragments of experience that present themselves in quite a different way.

The partial exceptions I have encountered are in visits to the diviner, where he provokes a response by asking what the problem is, and in accounts of past events in hearing dispute cases in moots and courts. However, in both instances narrative recollection is not elaborated into a complete life history but focussed on the situation in hand. The diviner will prompt questions from the client, which his paraphernalia of divining instruments will attempt to answer; in moots and courts we have more structured narrative accounts of the dispute, but directed to that incident, even though the notion of relevance may be more inclusive than is usual in a contemporary western court.

Narrativity, the narrative, above all the fictional narrative, does not seem to me a prominent characteristic of most oral cultures. The rise of narrative, anyhow of lengthy stories, is associated with written cultures. It is true that one finds, albeit very unevenly distributed, some recitations like that of the Bagre, but they are justified by their religious 'truth'. They can be regarded as fictional only in the same sense as the Old or New Testaments can be so considered.

This absence is not only a matter of the juvenile status of much fiction, of its imaginative relation with 'truth'. Part of the problem with long recitations is the attention they demand. The situation of an audience sitting round listening quietly to any long recitation seems to me a rare occurrence. Most discourse is dialogic; listeners react to what they hear, interrupting any long sequence. One may begin to listen for a short while to an individual's account of his voyage to Kumasi when he went to work down the mines or to another's story of a holiday in Mallorca. But he or she will not in real life be allowed to continue for long without some interruption, such as 'I myself had an experience like that'. The exception is when a monologue, because that is the nature of narrative, is validated by its supernatural character or context. One is hearing not about mundane matters but about 'the work of the gods'. So such 'mythical' accounts tend to be told in ritual contexts where attention is required for magico-religious reasons. It is ritual, ceremony, rather than narrative that is the focus of the recitation, which is often much less a purely storytelling exercise than the term narrative suggests – more like the diversity of discourse we find in the Bible. And in any case for the listener it is not fiction.

THE NOVEL

Walter Benjamin saw the advent of the novel as putting an end to storytelling (which he sees as basically a speech form), an end that began with the introduction of printing to Europe at the end of the fifteenth century. Lévi-Strauss considered that myth gave way to the novel at the beginning of the eighteenth century. My earlier argument has suggested that storytelling, at least to adults, and indeed narrative in general, received much less emphasis in pre-literate cultures than has been assumed. The break came with the coming of the written word. Writing takes place in private. We construct an autobiography, like a diary, in private. Privacy means that we do not face the problem of direct, unmediated communication to an audience, the problem of interruption or its authoritarian suppression; we have the peace and leisure to construct. Of course, later on the writing will probably become a public document. And in so doing it sets a model, an agenda, even for orally composed recollection of one's past. Literacy imposes its own pattern on the self-narrative and sets the stage for medical, sociological, psychological and analytic enquiries where the individual is asked to provide a 'history', a curriculum vitae. There is feedback from what the written has encouraged and achieved. Narratives, monologues, long recitations, are encouraged by writing. The products include some brands of fiction or fiction-like forms, such as epics of a heroic character or legends like saints' lives. The problems to which fictional narratives earlier gave rise in oral cultures are still there and that is perhaps one reason why the novel appeared so late on the scene, when printing was available to diffuse it, rather than with writing alone (though it is also present in the later classical period). When it does appear it signals the blossoming of narrative, which subsequently makes its mark in film and in the electronic media.

It is not difficult to see how narrative, the telling of true or fictional stories, was encouraged by writing. Writing automatically involves distance between the teller of tale and his or her audience in quite a different way from oral storytelling (which is necessary face-to-face). Both the teller and the reader have time to reflect upon what they are doing, either writing or reading, whereas the speaker is in immediate contact with the audience. A sheet of blank paper and a pen is an invitation to produce a narrative of structured recollections or of imaginative invention. One begins at the top of the page and continues to the foot, then goes on to the next. One is (relatively) uninterrupted in the writing as well as in the reading. Oral discourse does not work like that; a speaker is constantly being interrupted because except in authoritarian situations it is dialogic, interactive. From one point of view there is no real division between speaker and audience. All are speakers, all are listeners (of a kind) and the conversation proceeds in starts and stops, often in incomplete sentences and nearly always in unfinished narratives.

Of course, there are occasions in an oral culture when a speaker commands an authoritative position and delivers a continuous speech, either directed to a specific occasion or in a standard oral form (which would be 'literature' if written). These occasions are rare and special. Perhaps a traveller returning from a voyage and telling of his adventures and of the knowledge he has acquired. Or in politically centralized regimes, a chief or his spokesman addressing his subordinates gathered before him. Or a subject offering praise songs to the ruler, recalling the deeds of his ancestors, songs which perhaps verge on fiction.

Just as writing makes 'history' possible, so too it promotes life histories. I do not mean to imply that oral cultures have no conception of the past either on a societal or on a personal level, but organized, narrative history is rare, and without documents fragmentary. So in terms of cultural history, what is surprising about the novel, as distinct from narrative more generally, is not simply its absence from oral cultures, but its late and sporadic appearance long after writing was introduced, followed by its great popularity despite the continuing hostility it attracted up to the nineteenth century in Europe, later elsewhere. Today we live in a culture dominated by fiction, as none other has been.

The word novel appears to come into English from the Romance languages in the late fifteenth century with the meaning of news. Within ten years of the advent of the printing press to Europe, around 1486, Henry VII started to publish partisan diplomatic accounts as well as 'news' or announcements in occasional printed broadsheets. By Elizabeth's time various groups beside the government made use of this media, often for domestic affairs in the form of ballads. The term used for these news-ballads was *novels*, like the French *nouvelle* or the Spanish *novela*. 'It only suggested something new, and did not press the issue of facts versus fiction.'[32] In the sixteenth century the word is used, after the Italian, to refer to a tale or short story of the kind found in Boccaccio's *Decameron*. In the seventeenth century, it comes to be employed as in contemporary English to refer to a long fictional prose narrative in contrast to the romances (the French and Italian *roman*, *romanzo*, covers both), because of the close relation to real life. Nevertheless, the problem of acceptability remained. There was still a doubt, expressed by Steele in the *Spectator*,[33] when he wrote 'I'm afraid thy Brains are a little disordered with Romances and Novels'. The great diffusion of both was related to the mechanisation of writing in the form of printing, reducing the need to read aloud as many could acquire, even if temporarily from a friend or a library, their own copy for silent perusal.

It was this possibility of a disordered mind that encouraged the notion of people being led astray by fiction, the symptom of Bovarism named after Flaubert's nineteenth-century novel, but which had arisen much earlier with regard to the romances, in the many objections to the novel that were expressed in the eighteenth century, in the preference of most male readers for non-fiction and in the development of a dominantly female reading public.

The novel is clearly a product of literate cultures as well as of leisured ones, yet it flourished relatively late in cultural history and certainly did not follow on closely from the invention of writing itself. Early narratives appear in Greece and Rome, little in the earlier

[32] Sommerville 1996: 18.   [33] Steele 1711, number 254.

period in the Near East. But stories like Apuleius' *The Golden Ass* or Longus' *Daphne and Chloe* and the erotic romances of the Greeks were at best forerunners of the novel as we know it today.[34] Early examples of narrative fiction, often referred to as romances or novels, that were found in ancient Greek, Roman and Egyptian literature were relatively short, very different in scope from later novels either in Europe or in China. Although these works were thought to have been directed at a popular audience, the reading public was much smaller, more elitist, though it comprised women as well as men.[35] In Egypt fictional narratives were written in Demotic (from, say, the seventh century BCE), but they were apparently all 'of fairly modest length'. Modest could mean less than 6,000 words. Some were longer. 'The chief structural means by which stories were made more extensive than a simple anecdote is the device of a story-within-a-story.'[36] What kind of status did such fiction have? There is no evidence that narrative texts were used in education. Closer prototypes than these 'novels before the novel' appeared in Europe at the end of the Middle Ages, most notably in Rabelais and Don Quixote but also in the mass of French romances of the seventeenth century.

After the classical period and the long hiatus that followed in Europe, fiction seems to have revived only in the twelfth and thirteenth centuries. The historian N. Daniel sees this revival as representing a link with oral culture: 'The sudden appearance of a fictional literature is evidence of Europe's natural links with the other cultures that derive from the ancient sources of the Near East' – in other words, the Bronze Age cultures with their invention of writing.[37] For example, the earliest example of the 'boxed' story (the story within a story as in the *Arabian Nights*, the frame story for which is probably Indian and the first reference dates from the ninth century) he sees as being Pedro de Alfonso's *Discipline Clericalis*. The author was a converted Jew who translated the tale from the Arabic and 'was the first to introduce the genre of fable, a kind of subdivision of Wisdom literature'.[38]

Linked works of Indian origin such as Kalila wa Dimna and The Seven Sages [also known as 'the Book of Sinbad'] began to appear in the thirteenth

[34] On the novel in classical societies, see Perry 1967; Heisermann 1977; Hägg 1983; Tatum 1994; Morgan and Stoneman 1994; Holzberg 1995.
[35] Egger, 'Looking at Chariton's Callirhoe', in Morgan and Stoneman 1994.
[36] Tatum 1994: 206.   [37] Daniel 1975: 310.   [38] Daniel 1975: 108.

century [in Spain; in Greece in the eleventh century], and, a little later, Don Juan Manuel's *el Corde Lucaver*. European boxed stories include the *Confessio Amantis* of Gower, the *Novella* of Giovanni Sércambi (an important future name for the genre in English), Boccaccio (not only *Decameron* but also *Arreto*) and, above all, Chaucer's *Canterbury Tales*, as well as the *Tale of Bergis* associated for a time with Chaucer. All these date from the later fourteenth century and represent at least what we have called 'Mediterranean culture'; in some cases there are Arabic and even ultimately Indian sources.[39]

What is fascinating here is the relatively late appearance of these narrative forms at roughly the same period in different parts of the globe.

A central problem about the history of the novel is precisely its late arrival on the scene, its initially uneven distribution and its great and widespread popularity since the eighteenth century. The late arrival occurs not only in Europe but in China. Plaks remarks upon 'the outstanding coincidence that the rise of prose fiction occurs nearly simultaneously, step by step, in both China and Europe', namely, in the sixteenth century.[40] He tries to explain the appearance of the Ming literati novels, 'the four master-works', in terms of the transformation of the Ming economy, factional politics and the expanding educational system.[41] In other words, the form is certainly not a purely western phenomenon. While it is not found in all earlier literate societies, the limitation of the discussion of the rise of the novel to Europe, let alone to early eighteenth-century England, has no justification.

But why the uneven distribution and why the late arrival? I suggest the problem goes back to our earlier discussion of narrative, especially fictional narrative, in oral societies. Despite the development of narrative in writing, similar doubts about its fictional forms arose. Storytelling was always an ambiguous activity, implying 'telling a story' in the sense of an untruth or even a lie. It failed to represent reality, was not serious.

There were two ways around this problem. As with myth, the narrative could be legitimized in the form of an account of supernatural events, which automatically got around one objection to the reality of the representation. The earlier narratives of Christian Europe were legitimized as being accounts of heavenly miracles (the

---

[39] Daniel 1975: 310. [40] Plaks 1977: 321. [41] Plaks 1977: 6ff.

New Testament) or of the lives of saints, in the same way that painting and drawing became possible in the early Middle Ages if the subjects were drawn from religious sources. Even in the eighteenth century, it was this aspect of John Bunyan's *Pilgrim's Progress* that rendered it acceptable to many Nonconformist Protestants.

The modern novel, after Defoe, was essentially a secular tale, a feature that is contained within the meaning of 'realistic'. The hand of God may appear but it does so through 'natural' sequences, not through miracles or mirabilia. Earlier narrative structures often displayed such intervention which, in a world suffused by the supernatural, was present everywhere. Indeed, one can argue that in such circumstances the actors drew little distinction between natural and supernatural; it was certainly shaded, even in personal narratives. Those particular times had passed with the saints' tales and with the fantasy of the romance. And even earlier in the classical world, when there was a separation between the two, more distinct in some fields than in others.

With the coming of the Renaissance and of the printing press, secular romances made a strong appearance. But they were often ridiculed, seen as fare for leisured women rather than serious men, and having potentially very negative effects on their readers. With the eighteenth century in England, the romances of fantasy were supplemented by the realistic novels of Defoe and his followers, which were more serious and less fanciful.

The early eighteenth-century novel adopted a different strategy of legitimation, which was its claim to be true to life, to be 'a history' rather than a 'story'. Consider Defoe's attempts to establish the details of the time and place of the tale he is telling. And in fact the tale itself, in the case of *Robinson Crusoe* or *A Journal of the Plague Year*, did oscillate between truth and fiction, incorporating details of actual events. So too with time and place in Fielding or Smollett. The epistolary mode, adopted by Aphra Behn in the late seventeenth century and later by Samuel Richardson in *Clarissa*, was perhaps another example of this claim.

I have used the words 'truth', 'actual' and 'reality' in their obvious, literal, commonplace, perhaps superficial, meaning. There is an equally obvious sense in which these words could be applied to fiction that purported to say something imaginative about the human condition. But a discrimination between literal truth and poetic truth is often recognized and refers to different modes of discourse. Fictional narrative embodying the second is certainly promoted by the use of writing, but its fictional nature is sometimes concealed either by a concern with the supernatural, the non-natural or, in the early history of the novel, by the pretence to offer literal truth. In this way the reader's bluff is called, his or her doubts are calmed.

Despite the new realism in the eighteenth century, the novel was still heavily criticized. As fiction, it was widely considered to display a lack of seriousness, much as I have argued it did in many oral cultures. The resistance to the novel continued in eighteenth-century Europe, especially when this resistance formed part of what I have called 'the Puritanical Complex'.[42]

These objections to the novel and the preference for non-fiction are visible in the history of American printing. The first work in that category was the ambiguous production by Defoe, *The Dreadful Visitation in a Short Account of the Progress and Effects of the Plague … extracted from the Memory of a Person who Resided there*. This work, which as we now know was largely imaginative, was published in 1763 by Christopher Sauer of Germantown; *Robinson Crusoe* followed only twenty years later in 1774. New novels were imported from England; they were rare in the publishing world even of the later eighteenth century in America. For early New England firmly rejected the secular trends which it saw as returning with renewed vigour to England with the restoration of the Stuarts to the throne. The Puritans objected to idleness, to the theatre, to ribald literature. That included romances, which were seen as especially attractive to women. In 1693, Increase Mather wrote of this 'vast mischief of false notions and images of things, particularly of love and honour'. While such material was imported and diffused through circulating libraries, the moral arbiters continued to frown on all fiction.[43]

This resistance to fiction by important cultural authorities meant that its consumption and to some extent its production rested upon 'marginal' elements such as women. In seventeenth-century Europe, as we have recalled, the main readers of fiction were women; French romances were often written by women and it was women who

---

[42] Goody 2009b.   [43] Mather quoted in Daniels 1995: 46.

formed the main audience of the English novel in the eighteenth century. The dominance of women among the audience was one reason why it came under criticism. They were the ones more likely to be misled and deceived, especially by the lengthy romances, though not only them. The great Spanish novelist Cervantes built the picaresque novel *Don Quixote* around the deception of the hero who was led astray as the result of reading old romances.

It was the same in the eighteenth century. As we have noted, the 'realism' of the writings of Defoe and others was intended to contrast with these fanciful tales; they 'deceived' in another manner, by making false claims to historical truth as a way of presenting an imaginative tale that came closer to 'reality'. In this way they attempted to circumvent the criticism of the old romances that they misled people not only into false beliefs but into false conduct. The statement of this position is nowhere clearer than in Charlotte Lennox's *The Female Quixote*, in which she tells the story of Arabella who was herself misled by reading 'the great Store of Romances' left by her mother.

Such possibility of deception was not confined to the French and other romances; it was equally criticized for the Gothic novels of the later eighteenth century, above all by Jane Austen in *Northanger Abbey*. Q. D. Leavis emphasized 'how strong a part in Jane Austen's novels is played by her conscious war on the romance. She did to the romance of her day (whether the domestic romance of Fanny Burney or the Gothic brand of Mrs. Radcliffe) what Cervantes had done in his.'[44]

The heroine of the novel is Catherine Morland who strikes up a friendship with Isabella Thorpe in the Pump-room at Bath. The relationship between the two developed rapidly. When it was wet, they read novels together. 'Yes novels', declares the author,

– for I will not adopt that ungenerous and impolitic custom so common with novel writers, of degrading by their contemptuous censure the very performances, to the number of which they are themselves adding ... Let us leave it to Reviewers to abuse such effusions of fancy at their leisure, and to talk in threadbare strains of the trash with which the press now groans ... Although our productions have afforded more extensive and unaffected

---

[44] Kettle 1965: 112.

pleasure than those of any other literary corporation in the world, no species of composition has been more decried.

With this reputation, which the author herself discusses, Jane
Austen contrasts that of the *Spectator* or other non-fiction ('gentlemen
read better books').

All Catherine's experience came from reading fiction. She 'had read
too much not to be perfectly aware of the care with which a waxen
figure might be introduced [into the coffin], and a suppostitious
funeral carried on'. As with Don Quixote, with which the theme is
often compared, reading led her away from reality into 'fancy' (that
is, fantasy) which turned out to be 'folly'.

That reading coloured her entire journey to Northanger Abbey.
Nothing 'could shake the doubts of the well-read Catherine'; castles
and abbeys were 'the charm of her reveries' and with them went 'the
hope of some traditional legends, some awful memorials of an injured
and ill-fated nun'. Riding there in the curricle with her suitor, Henry
Tilney, she anticipated 'a fine old place, just like what one reads
about'. On this expectation he plays: 'Are you prepared to encounter
all the horrors that a building such as "what one reads about" may
produce?', going on to elaborate all the 'Gothic' possibilities of this
Gothic Abbey. Her responses were fully roused by the storm that
struck the building on her first night and by the closed chest and
cupboard which proved to contain nothing more than spare linen
and a laundry list. She suffered from 'causeless terror', from 'self-
created delusion', all due to the indulgence of that sort of reading.
For it was not in the works of Mrs Radcliffe that 'human nature, at
least in the midland counties of England, was to be looked for'.

Her suspicions were unfounded and Henry Tilney upbraided her.
'Remember that we are English, that we are Christians. Consult
your own understanding, your own sense of the probable, your
own observations of what is passing around you.' Not books but
your own experience. Her disillusion was complete. 'The visions of
romance were over, Catherine was completely awakened' 'from the
extravagances of her late fancies.'

The advocacy of 'critical realism' in *Northanger Abbey* is not
isolated.[45] Criticism of the novel, at least of the romantic and Gothic

---

[45] McKillop 1963: 52–61.

novel, appears in Maria Edgeworth's *Belinda*,[46] where Lady Delacour comments: 'My dear, you will be woefully disappointed, if in my story you expect anything like a novel.' In her early writings Jane Austen engages in burlesques that take the form of 'the direct inflation of the novel style'. In *Love and Friendship*,[47] Edward's father asks, 'Where Edward in the name of wonder did you pick up this unmeaning gibberish? You have been studying Novels, I suspect.' The genre came in for heavy criticism for being either a simulacrum or a travesty of life.

The best-known literary example of this kind of deception is undoubtedly Flaubert's *Madame Bovary* (1857); indeed, the predicament of the eponymous heroine has given rise to the problem of 'bovarism'. Her problem was not only being misled by novels but by reading in general. Like Don Quixote and Arabella, Emma Bovary is effectively 'in retirement', living in the country, married to a boring doctor and having little to do but lead a fantasy life of the imagination in which reading plays a dominant part. But her imagination revolves around contemporary life, not the past; she constructs a virtual reality for herself.

She bought herself a street map of Paris, and, with the tip of her finger, she went shopping in the capital.

She took out a subscription … to Le Sylphe des Salons. She devoured every single word of all the reviews of the first nights, race-meetings and dinner parties … She knew the latest fashions … she read Balzac and George Sand, seeking to gratify in fantasy her secret cravings. Even at the table, she had her book with her, and she would be turning the pages, while Charles was eating and talking to her. The memory of the Viscount haunted her reading. Between him and the fictional characters, she would forge connections.[48]

Emma used novels to escape from her own present into another imaginary existence. Books dominate her life. She entertains the young clerk, Leon, with the fashion magazines she has brought along. He 'sat beside her and they looked at the engraved plates together and waited for each other at the bottom of the page. Often she would ask him to read her some poetry …' 'And so between them arose a kind of alliance, a continual commerce in books and ballads …' When a certain novel starts a fashion for cactuses, he

⁴⁶ Edgeworth, M. 1801.   ⁴⁷ Austen, J. 1790.   ⁴⁸ Flaubert 1857: 45.

bought some for her in Rouen. The book overshadows all and directs much of the course of events for those who immerse themselves in it. This gives rise to a dependence on fiction, to a kind of addiction, to a devaluing of the life into which one was born and a hunger for a life of luxury, of a higher stratum. These qualities were thought to be characteristic of 'women in idleness', and a novelist portraying them reveals his own ambivalence towards the feminine; in criticizing them Flaubert is consciously playing with what he called his own feminine disposition.

These criticisms of the effects of fiction did not, of course, appear only within the pages of the novel itself. Already in 1666 Pierre Nicole, in *Visionnaires*, described 'a compiler of novels and a poet of the theatre' as 'a public poisoner'. One hundred years later Dr Pomme, in *Traité des affectives vapoureuses des deux sexes*,[49] suggests that among all the causes which have harmed the health of women, 'the principle has been the infinite multiplication of novels since a hundred years'. Concern about health continued. In 1900 La Baronne Staffe was still worrying about women in *Le Cabinet de toilette*. 'To remain, sitting, late into the night, reading novels, that's what produces around the eyes these terrible little marks that spoil the prettiest face.'

Moral health was even more at risk. In 1884 Gustave Claudin announced, 'It is above all the frivolous ladies who are the great readers of novels'; while as late as 1938 Jacques Leynon protests that soon every novel will have to have a chapter taking place in a brothel.[50] The Holy Book and Christian literature were approved. That was the fare of Roman ladies in the first centuries of Christianity, not the light novels of today, whose reading is so dangerous. Nor is their perusal confined to the towns: 'one encounters, in the country, the goat herd who has slid under her cape the bad romance already passed from hand to hand, and which she still had enough shame to want to hide'.

Why were criticisms of the novel and of fiction in general especially prevalent in Europe in the eighteenth century? That of course was the time when the genre took off, so that we could also expect it to be marked by pronounced resistance. It was also the period of the

---

[49] Dr Pomme 1767.
[50] These quotations are taken from Bechtel and Carrière 1984, for which reference I am indebted to Wolfgang Klein.

Enlightenment, of the new Encyclopedia, when many institutions were being queried. Criticisms of the novel, doubts about its legitimacy, were not confined to Europe, any more than the novel itself. Such objections lay at the root of its frequently marginal status and indeed of its failure to appear at all in many times and in many places. The early novel from eleventh-century Japan, *The Tale of Genji* by the Lady Murasaki, achieved a canonical status. Nevertheless, it attracted many objections, from Confucian scholars especially, due to 'its fictional character and … concentration on amorous relationships'.[51] In the Confucian tradition, the distrust of fiction is usually traced to a saying in *Analects*: 'The subjects on which the Master did not talk were extraordinary things, feats of strength, disorder, and spiritual beings.'[52] Fiction was among the genres of literature scorned by Confucian literati. McMullen comments: 'This distrust derives from the rational, didactic tenor of the tradition. Fanciful events strained credulity and lacked persuasive power. They were falsehoods, the products of undisciplined minds.'[53] This view is represented in the *Genji* itself. Indeed, the novel was defended by the great commentator of the early Tokugawa period, Banzan, as being a true record; it is not 'a bookful of lies'. Banzan adopted another line too, however, also found in Europe, justifying a genre where 'no fact exists but where a moral truth is comprehended and a fact supplied for it' – the underlying, imaginative or experiential truth.[54]

Similar criticisms arose wherever we find the novel, in China for example. The concept of *wen*, imitation, is discussed in the context of narrative literature, both historical and fictional. Indeed, the preferred form of fiction is often historical; the purely fictional is doubly suspect. As Plaks remarks, the act of fiction writing is 'the business of fabricating illusions of reality'; the opening formula of the 'Heart Sutra' that appears in *Jin Ping Mei* (*The Golden Lotus*) reads, 'reality is emptiness, emptiness is reality'.[55] The novels themselves offer criticisms of the way of life they describe, 'the fourfold scourges of excessive indulgence in wine, women, wealth and wrath'.[56] Indeed, the works themselves also contain some warnings about indulgence in

---

[51] McMullen 1999: 308.   [52] Quoted in McMullen 1999: 310.   [53] McMullen 1999: 310
[54] McMullen 1999: 315.   [55] Plaks 1977: 511–12.   [56] Plaks 1977: 505.

fiction. As in the eighteenth-century English novel, 'the simulated narrators' recurrent use of the rhetoric of historiography in introductory sections, asides, and concluding comments … to emphasize the sense of judgement going hand-in-hand with the mimetic presentation of events' may encourage the 'sense that the fictional narration may convey generalized truth even where it forgoes the presumption of historical veracity'.[57] Chinese literature has an important didactic component, often with Buddhist monks or Daoist recluses coming forward 'to preach what seems to be the author's own message of worldly renunciation', showing 'the futility of it all'. That moral message poses problems in the face of the manifest content often turning on 'excessive indulgence' and may lead to the introduction of warnings against fiction, at least in the hands of the young. That seems to have been more generally the view; the contents of novels were essentially frivolous, and indeed lewd and immoral. But there is a wider problem of truth and fiction which no amount of overlap (history/story) can entirely evade and which emerges in Confucian reactions, such as the criticisms of *The Tale of the Genji* in Japan. The balance that Plaks sees between the two also contains a contradiction which (under some circumstances) may lead to rejection as well as to acceptance.

Particular works might be suppressed for particular reasons. *Water Margin*, a tale of outlawry and rebellion, was thought to encourage brigands. Fiction and reality were merged; the work attacked the abuse of power and misgovernment, and is reformist in tone despite 'the anarchic actions of its heroes'. However, 'many late Ming peasant rebel leaders were taking the names or nicknames of *Water Margin* heroes for themselves'.[58] The authorities perceived this as a threat and ordered the work to be suppressed in 1642. The same happened to *The Merry Adventures of Emperor Yang*, not so much because of 'its explicit descriptions of the emperor's less conventional sexual exploits' but because it raised the question of the limits of loyalty.[59] *The Prayer Mat of Flesh* was 'more effectively proscribed'.[60]

This constellation of opposition to the novel recalls immediately the similar set of societies I have discussed elsewhere regarding

---

[57] Plaks 1977: 328.   [58] Hegel 1981: 77.   [59] Hegel 1981: 85.
[60] Hegel 1981: 227.

opposition to images and to the theatre, as well as to relics (bones) and flowers.[61] The suspicion that we are dealing with a general phenomenon is again strengthened. It is strengthened still further when we look at recent events in China where again we find the suppression of flowers, of religious (and other) images and of the theatre. The novel shares in this history. In the Sichuan town of Yebin during the Cultural Revolution, Jung Chang's mother initially had a hard time in her party cell, being subject to continual criticism. But when she was moved to a new job and a new cell, things were better: 'Instead of sniping at her like Mrs Mi, Mrs Tung let my mother do all sorts of things she wanted, like reading novels; before, reading a book without a Marxist cover would bring down a rain of criticism about being a bourgeois intellectual'.[62]

In Islam and in Judaism objections seem to have gone deeper. The former made a firm distinction between historical truth and religious myths on the one hand, and imaginative fiction on the other. Such storytelling might be used, as in *The Thousand and One Nights*, to distract, but it consisted essentially of a distraction from more serious activities. In the Arab world there were general objections to affabulation in historical and exegetical work, and occasional and casual expression of contempt from a learned standpoint was directed at the *Arabian Nights*. But such tales were not only read before plebeian audiences; they seem to have been in favour at court, especially those containing mirabilia, like the voyages of Sinbad. Once again objections to fiction, ambivalences to created narrative, seem to be rooted in the fact that it 're-presents' reality and is not itself the truth. Even serious narrative may be looked down upon as a way of discovering truth more appropriate for children and for those who need guidance than for the sophisticated searcher, rather like icons for early Christians and for Buddhists.

Later in nineteenth-century Europe such criticism was more muted. That was when fiction came into its own with the reading public, with the great novelists, Scott, the Brontes, Dickens, Eliot, Meredith and Trollope, in England. This dominance of the novel has been seen as deeply transforming human emotions and behaviour. While that may be partially true, it is also accused of making such

---

[61] Goody 1997.   [62] Chang 1991: 26.

behaviour more shallow, as the result of copying the actions of the characters in 'romances'. That was a constant criticism of the eighteenth century and remained true in the nineteenth when Madame Bovary was seduced away from 'reality' by its fictions, indeed by reading itself. The defence again lay in its role in peering below the surface at the 'underlying truth' of the novel, at least of the distinguished novel. But that approach provided no defence at all against the bulk of fiction, whether of Mills and Boon, of Dame Barbara Cartland, or of most detective series, thrillers and westerns which are frankly 'escapist', as is most film and television. That movement certainly represents a major shift over the past hundred years or so. Until the mid nineteenth century, most published books were theological in character. If they read at all, most men read serious non-fictional works, whereas fiction was left largely to women to read, and sometimes to create. The situation began to change with the historical romances of Scott, and today the readership of the novel is no longer gendered in the same way, although certain types may well be.

This form has today become completely accepted as a genre, largely immune from the earlier criticism. Indeed, the phrase 'criticism of the novel' has acquired a totally different meaning as the genre has moved from the shadows to a dominant position on the literary scene. In the same period, the image was diffused in every corner of society through printing, and iconoclasm virtually disappeared, so overwhelming was its presence. Something of the same process seems to have occurred with fiction; objections were drowned out by the sheer quantity coming off the press and the incorporation of the novel into daily life. Nevertheless, the contradictions, which, as I have argued elsewhere, are inherent in the process of representation, still found occasional expression. Even in the sphere of the visual arts, where the revival of both painting and sculpture long preceded the dominance of the novel, opposition has continued. Walter Benjamin called attention to the recent victory of the visual arts (perhaps especially noticeable for a Jew as for a Puritan) and he attributed this to the tidal wave of cheap publications made available by changes in the modes of communication. Nevertheless, resistance continued, at least in the visual domain, taking shape in the works of French abstract painters. For them the represented object was merely the superficial manifestation of a more profound truth, an essence, a purity, that could be expressed only in the absence of objects, of figurative representation, of iconicity. Perhaps the same kind of resistance to pictorial representations also takes the contemporary shape of preserving the carcass of a sheep in formaldehyde; only the real thing is truth, never the still life, *nature morte.*

Did the same process occur with fictional representations? There have been a number of attempts at the anti-novel, and radical efforts to reorganize it on less narrative lines. James Joyce, Virginia Woolf, others too, *le nouveau roman*, have made moves in this direction. Basically the storytelling form has endured, filling the windows of our bookshops and the news-stands of our railways and airports. But in art, abstraction and repression of 'reality' had their roots in the late impressionists and reached their apogee in Russia with Malevich and Kandinsky, with their philosophical justifications for the abstract as attaining purity of vision. Was the dominance of the novel, at least at the popular level, partly due to its changing content, that is, to the elaboration of specifically sexual themes (for example, in the romantic novel) and of the murder mystery (in the detective story)? Both of these topics were often suppressed in earlier literature. Love was not eliminated but sex was, except in Chinese novels such as *Jin Ping Mei* and in the erotic novels of ancient Greece, and that too was the situation in seventeenth- and eighteenth-century Europe.

This point raises the question of how far storytelling is linked to seduction. In *Othello*, the Moor claims he attracted Desdemona, the daughter of a Venetian senator, by his tales of foreign lands, of

> The Anthropophagi, and men whose heads
> Did grow beneath their shoulders. (1.3.143–4)

Nevertheless,

> She'd come again, and with a greedy ear
> Devour up my discourse (lines 148–9)

He concludes 'She loved me for the dangers I had passed' (line 166). Telling a story, creating one's fictional biography or personal life, is part of many a courting encounter. The story and its telling seduces or prevents seduction, as with Shaharazad and Sinbad.

The change to mass novel-reading represents a shift of interest to one in which the majority were concerned with 'entertainment', with distraction, after their time at school or university. The sales figures for books amply illustrate the different perspective, and that has to be regarded as a change of consciousness. It is true that individuals now read more newspapers, more 'serious' journalism, probably more biographies and autobiographies and that their knowledge of the world is more profound than in earlier times. But so too is their desire for entertainment, especially 'home entertainment', made possible by the relative cheapness of reading matter and by the installation of the radio, television and the computer in the home, bringing there fiction, film as well as 'the news' and commentaries, including the public discussions of contemporary issues.

With the novel, one hears complaints of triviality, of escapism, rather in the same vein as the eighteenth century saw fiction as more appropriate for women in their domestic capacities than for men working in the outside world. Today, biography is perhaps more masculine, more concerned with the world. Can the novel, offering an imaginative version of experience, ever compete with the reality of everyday life, especially in the aftermath of the Holocaust? That at least is the problem raised by the novelist Wolfgang Holdesheimer, an interpreter at the Nuremberg trials. In a lecture in Dublin in 1981, he predicted the end of the novel since fiction was incapable in his eyes of taking stock of the complexities of our age, in particular of the horrors of mass extermination. There are topics with which imaginative fiction cannot expect to deal.

In summary my argument runs as follows. Narrative, and in particular fictional narrative, is not a predominant characteristic of adult intercourse in purely oral (non-literate) cultures. Long narrative sequences, whether fictional or not, require special discourse situations. Short fictional narratives, or folktales, are aimed mostly at children – adults already know 'Cinderella' and do not need it repeated, partly because the content is clearly aimed at a juvenile audience. Longer recitations, in which the narrative element is rarely the most prominent, require a ritual setting to provide an attentive audience for whom the hearing may be something of an 'ordeal', and require a validation from beyond the human realm. Contrary to many beliefs, the epic is characteristic not of oral cultures (though it may be presented in speech) but of early literate ones. That was also, in the writer's view, the case with Homer and the Indian epics.[63]

The reason for the scarcity of long fictional narratives is different from that for long recitations in general. As with shorter folk-tales, the former may be recognized as trivial, fit for children and for distraction, as compared with the weightier demands of truth. In other words, their scarcity is related to the inherent problem in representations of all kinds pointed out by Plato, but in no sense limited to the western tradition, that fiction is not historical (self-evident) truth; it is from the literal point of view a lie, although it may aim at another kind of imaginative truth. Aim at but not necessarily succeed in achieving. And for some that aim will always remain illusory; the biography, which doubtless contains its element of make-believe, may be preferred to the invented story, which may offer only a distraction, not a 'truth' of any kind.

In real life the narrative is rarely unchallenged. The legal/jural process is perhaps the touchstone since the narrative is part of the duel, the plaintiff tells his story, the defendant another; one is judged to be truthful, the other a lie (or at least is not to be believed).

Doubts about fiction, about the novel, have dogged the history of this genre, because such worries are embedded in the human situation. With the dominance of 'fictionality' in Europe since the eighteenth century, as it became so central a feature of life with the advent of printing, of the rotary press, and finally of the electronic media, with the cinema and with television, resistance to fiction and the novel has become less explicit. Nevertheless some tension remains.

For fiction is the domain of fancy and fantasy. The sharp contrast between fancy and reality is a key theme of the poems of John Keats. Fancy is highly praised in the poem of that name.[64]

> Ever let the Fancy roam,
> Pleasure never is at home;
> At the touch sweet Pleasure melteth,
> Like to bubbles when rain pelteth;

---

[63] Goody 1987.   [64] Keats 1818.

Fancy can step in when life disappoints.[65] But it only does so in a deceptive (lying) way, as we are told in the final stanza of the 'Ode to a Nightingale'.

> Forlorn! the very word is like a bell
> To toll me back from thee to my sole self!
> Adieu! the fancy cannot cheat so well
> As she is fam'd to do, deceiving elf.

My interest in narrative, especially fictional narrative, arises from my interest in representations. Narrative itself, I argue, is not as pervasive as many recent accounts suggest, certainly not in purely oral cultures. When one thinks of it, life does not proceed like a sequential narrative. It is full of repetitions (the breakfast menu, the embrace on parting) which would make little narrative sense. The narrative, but not the sequence in a looser sense, is broken by knocks on the door, by the next e-mail message (one is bleeping its way through as I write), by scarcely relevant thoughts. Hence the stream of consciousness may be a closer representation of reality than the narrative, which I am using with a tighter meaning than just sequence.

Fiction as distinct from narratives of actual events adds another dimension. At the surface level it is plainly not 'true', though it may claim to be so. So in this sense it is a lie, as Plato maintained of the arts in general. To re-present was not to present; it embodied an illusion. It was this doubt, lying at the core of the arts, that led not only to criticism of their achievements but at times to their virtual banishment. To this I attribute the background historical fact of the virtual disappearance of the great artistic achievement of the classical world, sculpture, three-dimensional representation, and even two, certainly in a secular context, during the European Middle Ages. So too representation in the form of the theatre vanished from the scene. Physically the theatre collapsed; indeed, in St Albans and elsewhere it seems to have been deliberately destroyed early in the fourth century CE and did not reappear except in temporary form for some 1,500 years.

---

[65] On the concept of Fancy and its role in social life there is of course Dickens, *Hard Times* (1854).

There are two aspects to these absences and doubts. The first expresses a reaction to the 'luxuries' of post-Bronze Age culture, to the emergence of the stage, to the development of aesthetic activities such as reading novels, painting pictures, which were enjoyed mainly by the few, who had the leisure, education and motivation to participate. These luxury cultures were differentiated hierarchically in material and cultural terms. That situation often gave rise to some kind of ideological and practical opposition, expressed most clearly by moralists, philosophers and theologians. But there is a second problem inherent in representation itself and therefore in fiction.

Any form of re-presentation may raise doubts and hence ambivalence about its relationship with the original. Such doubts I suggest are inherent in the human situation of language-using animals facing their environment. It is intrinsic to language, and therefore to narrative. A horse (word) is never a horse (animal). An account of events is never the events themselves. When it does not even pretend to be such an account but is fictional, the situation is aggravated, even when it claims an underlying 'truth'. It is I think because of these general Platonic objections, reinforced in post-Bronze Age cultures by parallel 'puritanical' tendencies which are generally constructed around the rejection of luxury, that fiction including the novel has had the history and the distribution that has marked it worldwide. Even in oral cultures fiction is largely assigned to children, and until recently raised widespread doubts for adults, above all for those concerned with the running of society.

Writing modifies some of those doubts; fiction and narrative expand. But doubts persist, even today where the genre has become dominant, and there remains a substantial divide between entertainment and more 'serious' writing, between fiction and non-fiction.

CHAPTER 9

Writing and oral memory: the importance of the 'lecto-oral'

The final chapter treats of the difference that writing makes to oral memorization. The practice of learning things 'by heart' seems to be a feature of written cultures, where sentences can be read over and over again, without variations, where you can learn to recite the Bible in a different way from the constantly changing Bagre.

With writing there is clearly the propensity to take over some activities hitherto carried out in the oral tradition and hence to change their character and their consequences. It is clear that when writing is introduced into a society there is at once an opening up of some new spheres of communication and a replacement of old ones by this new medium. I mean, for example, by 'new spheres' that a whole new mode of schooling and instruction is opened up, using writing boards, blackboards or textbooks as a basis for teaching, and creating a new institution, the school, and new personnel, the teachers, as well as their counterparts, the pupils (usually children). At the same time, indigenous forms of socialization inevitably suffer. Learning to live in society is partially removed from direct participation with kin and transferred to the classroom and the teacher. Obviously this change reduces communication between parent and child, which is predominantly by word of mouth in any culture, and increases the element of writing and reading, which is what school is primarily about. It is a shift that comes with the very beginning of writing, which demands school-type situations for instructional purposes – often even among simple, locally invented scripts such as the Vai of West Africa, though more recently this skill seems unusually to have been passed down among kinsfolk.[1]

---

[1] Scribner and Cole 1981.

Where refinement over time makes a difference is in the development of scripts and of reading aids. While writing itself emerged in Mesopotamia using a logographic script, the alphabet obviously made writing simpler (after the initial difficulty of breaking the code), although there were advantages in the logographic where second languages were involved. Compare the quantity (and quality) of writing produced by Greek scholars working with a complete alphabet (or even Hebrew ones working with a consonantal one) to that produced in cuneiform. It represented a development of much more fluid forms.

As for replacement of the oral with the literate, the oral prayers made to shrines are now largely replaced with written ones, such as the Lord's Prayer or parallels in Islam. They are fixed. So in a sense one can say this leads to a retreat from cultural areas where orality once held sway, less spontaneity. These changes made possible the development of long narrative genres like the novel, which required freedom of writing and of the faculty to read. The novel began in the late classical period but its real development only took place with the mechanization of writing that occurred with the invention of the printing press, eventually permitting the cheap reproduction of long texts, and which set up very different relationships between an author and reader, between seller and buyer, than had previously existed. In these respects, as in many others, what one might call refinements in the script do contribute something not only to the opening up of new spheres but to the replacement of old ones. In the case of the narrative, the whole genre was radically changed. Folktales told in oral contexts were not so much replaced, they continued with children in the nursery, but they were now supplemented by long fictional stories of a new and quite different type. Indeed, the development of narrative itself, often seen as an art of oral cultures, was undoubtedly encouraged by the invention of writing and later of printing. The African novel emerged in a post-colonial context when largely oral cultures were being transformed, in their communicative practices, in their relationship between storyteller and audience, by the adoption of writing and of the printed word.

The situation was not fundamentally different with religious texts. The major works of world religions – the Old Testament of the Jews, the New Testament of the Christians, the Quran of the

Muslims, parallel texts in Mazdaism, in Hinduism and Buddhism – were inevitably products of written cultures. And they differ from the recitation of purely oral cultures in two important ways. Firstly, they are much longer; secondly, they are consistent over time and space. We do find some long recitations in oral cultures, such as the Myth of the Bagre. The first I wrote down ('The First Bagre') was of almost Homeric proportions (the latter being, in my no doubt minority opinion, a written text and composed as such). But later versions I recorded and transcribed were by no means as long, and that raises the second point of consistency. With writing, we arrive at the possibility of a canonized text that has consistency over time and place. This is not at all the case with the Bagre which varies with every recitation, less so when the same reciter (Speaker, as I call him) is involved but even then there are substantial changes, innovations as well as forgettings, with every performance.

Now this process of the canonization of a long written (religious) text does not come immediately with writing; the corpus develops over time and is perhaps more a feature of alphabetic literacy rather than of logographic scripts. It was a development (like the novel) not only of writing per se, not only of 'instant literacy', but of a historical development of scripts and of the written tradition, of what is handed down and elaborated and organized in writing or in print.

But we have to be very careful when we talk about the decline in oral transmission. That can mean two things: a decline compared to transmission in purely oral cultures and a decline in the orally transmitted component in societies with writing, what I call specifically 'the oral tradition' or the lecto-oral. For it must be remembered that the arrival of a new means of communication does not replace the earlier (except in certain limited spheres), it adds to it and alters it. Speech adds to gesture, writing to speech, the electronic media to writing. And as humanity develops, it uses an increasing number of channels of communication, the later ones always assuming the presence of the earlier. Mother–child communication is never done in writing, if only because the child does not yet know letters. Initially all human communication, even in cultures with writing, is made in the oral register. There can be no decline there; indeed, literate parents probably communicate orally more frequently with their children than non-literates, or those with less training in literacy (education).

That is one way in which children's language skills, eventually to be expressed in writing (at least in most cases), are encouraged.

A similar situation has existed at the societal level throughout human history, until the last hundred years or so, because all cultures, ever since writing was invented, have been split into two groups, into two subcultures, the one consisting of those who could read and the other of those who could not. So a great deal of communication with one's fellow human beings had to take place through speech rather than writing.

These are 'forced' situations, communications between literates and illiterates. But it is also the case with adults in families or with colleagues in the office or factory; communication by way of the written mode would be looked down upon as being unnecessarily formal or bureaucratic. Oral (lecto-oral) transmission prevails among those who are close and there has been no decline here with the adoption of writing for other tasks involving communication at a distance.

But, of course, the fact that oral transmission has been retained in these areas does not mean that the content is uninfluenced by the written word. Far from it. Speech is influenced in its pronunciation, its syntax and in its content. The content of the tales a mother tells her child may well be derived from a written source, such as Perrault's *contes de fées*, or even from the Quran itself. That is the case all along the line. Of course, the process of transmission differs greatly from that in a purely oral society, since with a written text the reciter (the mother, for example) can always refer back to the original and correct the story that she has told, a process that is quite impossible in purely oral cultures where the items have to be held in memory or not at all. And in memory that is not all that perfect from a verbatim point of view.

Here I want to refer to one rather curious feature of oral transmission in literate cultures which emphasizes not so much a decline as a revolution in 'orality'. The advent of writing does away with the necessity of memorizing long texts. Indeed, in purely oral cultures it would be virtually impossible to remember a long work like the Quran, even if one could visualize it as an oral product (which would be impossible). Even short ones may be committed to memory in ways that would generally be regarded as strange in those oral cultures. For example, in the first schools in Mesopotamia, the students had to write down their lesson on one side of a clay tablet, then turn the tablet over so the writing was hidden and thus reproduce the text. In other words, the writing was used as a tool to develop the memory, of lists of objects, for example, at a time when writing made the exact memorizing of those lists unnecessary. Indeed, this process created the task itself, since with a written text you could look back at it again and again and get it absolutely right, as we do with the Lord's Prayer, in a way that I suggest is virtually non-existent in purely oral cultures, except for very short passages. Nor is it necessarily valued as an achievement in oral cultures to reproduce a passage exactly, mechanically one might say, in this fashion. Yet it becomes a valued goal in written cultures, even with very long texts such as the Quran or the Bible that are often deliberately committed to memory by those who have learned to read and write even though the advent of writing has objectively rendered such a store quite unnecessary. By this process, they internalize the word of God. As a consequence, religious recitations of oral cultures, such as the Bagre today, may no longer vary with every performance. Writing has frozen the text. However, that text is committed to memory and then recited as if it were an oral product. An extraordinary effort was made in religious schools (and most early schools were religious) to memorize such texts. Partly, as in Mesopotamia, this was because written knowledge did not properly exist unless, like knowledge in oral cultures, it was internalized, actually made part of the body internally as well as the tablet externally. Even today we may act as if this were the case. 'Knowing a poem' is often understood as being able to recite that composition 'by heart'. Knowledge is largely bound up with memory, with oral presentation. With the written text, the author may have copied from a book; he or she may not really *know* the subject. Indeed, much early written scholarship has very much that quality, not simply of referring to another text but of incorporating it wholesale, in other words, of being plagiaristic.

This is the principle on which most of our examinations are built up. We know French when we know the word for 'immigrant', not when we know where to look it up in the dictionary. We know history when we can reproduce dates or discussions about the French Revolution, not when we know where to look it up in Furet, Ozouf or the *Encyclopaedia*

Universalis. For this purpose, the *Encyclopaedia Britannica* is seen as an aid to memory where the information has been stored. We have to 'learn' the 'facts' and then regurgitate them, possibly in an oral examination but most likely in a written one where, as in Mesopotamian schools, we are not allowed to consult the written original (that would be 'cheating') but only our own 'oral' memories, our storage systems.

Of course, there are some contexts in which this process of internalizing the written word so that we 'know' (memorize) what is there without consultation is of fundamental importance, as with the instructions on the bottle of medicine or those telling us how to work an electronic device. It is especially true of certain devices which are basic to further operations and which may be said to derive from a refinement of knowledge embodied in the script rather than the script itself (though this latter aspect does enter into consideration). I refer here to the alphabet itself. With the alphabet, we have an arbitrary arrangement of vowels and consonants, ABC, which it is essential to memorize by heart in a particular order so that one can use it for purposes such as indices. It is an order that was passed down unchanged in literary and spoken forms for several millennia. So too with the signs used for mathematics. Once again the order and their elementary multiplication has to be learnt by heart; so that we can then perform mental or written operations on which calculation is based it is essential to learn signs in a certain order. In these two cases we need to do this so that further operations can be undertaken which are virtually impossible in a purely oral mode; however, that is not necessarily the case for illiterates in a society with writing since they too can learn to operate these devices of intellectual technology, even without knowing how to read and write, as they can acquire them by the spoken word from somebody who can.

One problem about this mediated use of orality is discovering how somebody 'knows' something (or some topic) if he or she does not commit it to memory and then regurgitates it for the benefit of examiners. How can we ascertain if he or she has attended school, listened to lectures, and understood what the teacher has said if we do not employ some such testing mechanism?

The answer depends, partly at least, on how we later want to use that knowledge. If we want to speak to a native of France, then we need to internalize (remember) our knowledge of French words. If we want to translate for publication, then that sort of knowledge is unnecessary. And one has known very accomplished translators who are incapable of speaking the language in question. With some other subjects, internalized knowledge is less necessary, if you know how to make a diagnosis with the aid of the internet (or a medical textbook) or if you know where to look up the 'facts' about Kosovo in the encyclopedia.

Learning to recite by heart a long religious text such as the Quran or the Bible is not the equivalent of learning these technologies of the intellect, devices that are essential for further learning, for 'learning to learn'. In the first place they take up a great deal of time at schools, which could be devoted to other activities. Take many traditional Islamic primary schools where learning to recite the Quran may devour all a pupil's time, leaving none to acquire other forms of knowledge, committing to memory something that was already available in a written form – a different and more accurate mode of storage. That meant the students had to spend a large part of their time in memorizing a text, in verbatim repetition, in learning to recite (in the literal sense) by heart rather than in acquiring other forms of knowledge. This is what I have elsewhere called 'restricted literacy' since the ability to read is at first confined to religious texts. And religious texts, if they are the word of God, contain the whole truth. Of course, the pupils may learn 'to read' in a sense, except that in many cases they do not learn to read freely but only to recite the text from certain mnemonics. That is the same with much learning in the *yeshiva*, the religious schools of the Jewish tradition, where scholars can be seen standing at desks, swaying backwards and forwards, as they learn to recite the text for later repetition. The same was true of many early Christian schools, and, even in eighteenth-century France, Furet and Ozouf[2] write of a system in rural areas that taught pupils little more than to recite the Creed. It was only in the institutions of advanced learning that one sometimes progressed from this type of instruction to something more creative, more exploratory, an opportunity that was only open to the very few, especially under a hegemonic religion.

[2] Furet and Ozouf 1977.

As we have seen, this 'pretence at orality' is generally associated with religious texts. That process now seems strange to us, but it is a feature of literacy. In the first five thousand years of written civilizations, most reading and writing was learned in temples, churches, mosques; the instructors were priests and they inevitably used religious texts as a major part of their instruction. The partial exceptions were ancient Greece and China, societies which did not subscribe to a single written religion in the way that was characteristic of the Near East (and its religions) and of India. In those areas, a greater freedom was available in the educational process that had some influence on the subject matter used and discussed. Otherwise, literacy seems to have been restricted, especially for the masses.

Even in ancient Greece, the text of Homer was committed to memory in similar fashion; so too with the Vedas, though there is little doubt that both already existed in written form. For that mode of learning was by no means confined to the Near East. As a written text, the Rig Veda became the subject of intensive rote learning by the Brahmans, who were taught to recite it in their schools so that they could deliver the work orally without recourse to the original. That was their aim. The intervention of most Brahman priests in rituals is confined to their reading or recitation of a fixed text. Secular knowledge is less likely to be treated in such a manner. Was Aristotle ever memorized like this? But, as we have seen, there are still pressures to make us memorize and therefore be able to reproduce orally what has been written in books. Just as there are pressures on speech makers not to read their contributions to a debate but at worst to consult notes since it seems more genuine, more true, more convincing, if the words come straight from the speaker's heart rather than read from a script.

There is some change in the role of written texts over time. We have the development of literary forms such as novels, the words of which are scanned rather than internalized, at least in a verbatim sense. They are associated with rapid reading. Scanning also applies to works of non-fiction, especially to philosophical or scientific texts like those of Aristotle in ancient Greece which are read for their 'meaning', their 'essence', their 'ideas', rather than learnt by heart. You no longer articulate speech, the words of the language, you scan them visually. And that very important process for the development of cognitive processes seems to imply a certain decline in oral transmission *pari passu* with the 'refinement' of the uses of writing, rather than the written system itself.

This process of scanning a text, of rapid reading, was, however, accompanied by what can be considered more specifically as refinements of the written system. There was, of course, the standardization of spelling that accompanied the invention of printing. And of great importance was the development of a standard set of orthographic tools that permitted the clear and unambiguous interpretation of texts, when the word no longer had the support of orality, of voice, of emphasis, of gesture, of movement of the face and arms. In the alphabetic writing system we inherited from the classical period, we developed ways of indicating the breaks between words, sentences, paragraphs and chapters, of marking the beginning and the end of letters, of showing questions and direct speech.

In conclusion, while the refinement, even the existence, of writing does something to diminish the importance of oral tradition, it also sometimes encourages orality (the 'lecto-oral') in the context of a written one by continuing to view 'real' knowledge as knowledge which though in origin written has to be produced orally on demand. This is especially true of religious knowledge but includes the secular too in the context of school and college education. Moreover, one has to remember that reading aloud was until quite late the main form of reading. Even for one's own edification or enjoyment the text was turned into oral (lecto-oral) communication. So in retrospect, writing and the refinements of the text did not always lead to a decline in orality; literacy, it might be said, made people almost even more verbal.

APPENDIX

Folktales in northern Ghana

Table 1. *Characters in LoDagaa stories: animals*

Elephant	Leopard	Lion	Hyena	Duiker	Buffalo	Crocodile
8	9	8	11	4	10	2
Monkey	Fox	Wild boar	Squirrel	Rabbit	Tortoise	Toad
4	1	1	2	5	5	6
Lizard	Snake	Bat	Mouse	Rat	Bird	Hawk
3	5	1	1	2	11	1
Fly	Mason wasp	Bee	Lice	Ant	Spider	Fish
3	1	3	1	4	24	2
Donkey	Horse	Goat	Ram	Dog	Cat	Chicken
2	3	6	1	6	3	4

N = 79

Table 2. *Characters in Gonja stories: animals*

Elephant	Leopard	Lion	Hyena	Duiker	Chameleon	Buffalo
9	7	14	17	2	7	14
Crocodile	Monkey	Fox	Wild boar	Squirrel	Rabbit/Hare	Tortoise
1	13	3	3	1	4	9
Toad	Lizard	Snake	Bat	Rat	Bird	Hawk
1	4	4	1	2	17	2
Fly	Mason wasp	Spider	Scorpion	Firefly	Donkey	Horse
1	2	43	1	4	3	2
Goat	Ram	Dog	Cat	Chicken		
6	4	10	2	5		

N = 114

Table 3. *Characters in Gonja and LoDagaa stories compared: animals (percentage of stories containing animals)*

	Spider	Scorpion	Mason wasp	Firefly	Fly	Ant
Gonja	36	1	1	1	1	–
LoDagaa	30	–	1.3	–	4	5

	Lice	Bee	Bird	Hawk	Elephant	Leopard	Lion
Gonja	–	–	5	2	7.5	6	12
LoDagaa	1.3	4	14	1.5	10	11	10

	Hyena	Buffalo	Duiker	Crocodile	Monkey	Fox
Gonja	14	11	2	1	11	2
LoDagaa	14	12.5	5	2.5	5	1.3

	Wild boar	Chameleon	Squirrel	Tortoise	Rabbit/Hare
Gonja	2.5	6	1	7.5	3.3
LoDagaa	1.3	–	2.5	6.3	6.3

	Toad	Lizard	Snake	Bat	Mouse	Rat
Gonja	1	3.3	3.3	1	–	2
LoDagaa	7.5	4	6.3	1.3	1.3	2.5

	Horse	Donkey	Goat	Ram	Dog	Cat	Chicken
Gonja	2	2.5	5	3.3	8	2	7.5
LoDagaa	4	2.5	7.5	1.3	7.5	4	5

Gonja N = 114; LoDagaa N = 79

Table 4. *Characters in LoDagaa stories: humans*

Chief	Chief's wife	Chief's son	Chief's daughter
12	1	3	2
Boy	Girl	Woman	Man
17	10	20	20
Hunter	Shepherd	Brother	Wife
11	1	2	5
Blind man	Leper	Lame man	Witch
3	8	1	5

N = 79

Table 5. *Characters in Gonja stories: humans*

Chief		Chief's daughter	Hunter	Man/Father	Woman/Mother	
10		4	8	8+12 (20)	9+24 (33)	
Boy	Girl	Child	In-law	Leper	War chief	Adam
20	7	19	4	2	1	2
Eve	Abraham	Grand-mother	Farmer	Villager	Chief's household	
1	1	3	1	2	1	

N = 114

Table 6. *Characters in Gonja and LoDagaa stories compared: humans (percentage of stories containing humans)*

	Chief	Chief's wife	Chief's son	Chief's daughter
Gonja	8	–	–	3
LoDagaa	15	1.3	4	2.5

	Chief's household	War chief	Farmer	Villager	Hunter
Gonja	1	1	1	24	6
LoDagaa	–	–	–	–	14

	Shepherd	Blind man	Leper	Lame man	Witch	Man/Father
Gonja	–	–	2	–	–	16
LoDagaa	1.3	4	10	1	6.3	25

	Woman/Mother	Boy	Girl	Child	In-law
Gonja	28	16	6	15.5	43
LoDagaa	25	22	12.5	–	–

	Wife	Brother	Grand-mother	Adam	Eve	Abraham
Gonja	–	–	2.5	1	1	1
LoDagaa	6.3	2.5	–	–	–	–

Gonja N = 114; LoDagaa N = 79

Table 7. *Characters in LoDagaa stories: gods*

God	God's Son	Fairy	Ghost*
7	2	6	2

*In addition, there is one story involving a Mr Large-eyes and a Mr Long-hands; another involved a magic pot.

Table 8. *Characters in Gonja stories: gods*

God*	Fairy	Ghost
16*	4	1

*In one story, A.D. 7, God is shown as Chief/Chief God and hence is not included; this has to be checked.

Table 9. *Characters in Gonja and LoDagaa stories compared: gods (percentage of stories containing gods)*

	God	God's Son	Fairy	Ghost
Gonja	12	–	3	1
LoDagaa	8.8	2.5	7.58	2.5

Table 10. *Categories of characters in Gonja and LoDagaa stories*

	Humans only	Gods only	Animals only	All three
Gonja	11	–	28	10

	Humans and gods	Humans and animals	Animals and gods
Gonja	3	52	5

	Humans only	Gods only	Animals only	All three
LoDagaa	14	–	16	3

	Humans and gods	Humans and animals	Animals and gods
LoDagaa	8	32	4

N/A Gonja = 5; total N = 114
N/A LoDagaa = 2; total N = 79

References

Auden, W. H. 1994 *Collected Poems*, ed. E. Mendelson. London
Austen, J. [1790] 2003 *Love and Friendship*. London
   1817 *Northanger Abbey*. London
Bâ, A. H. and Kesteloot, L. (eds.) 1969 *Kaïdara*. Paris
Bartlett, F. 1932 *Remembering*. Cambridge
Barth, F. 1987 *Cosmologies in the Making: a generative approach to cultural variation*. Cambridge
Bechtel, G. and Carrière, J.-C. 1984 *Dictionnaire de la bêtise et des erreurs de judgement*. Paris
Bellah, R. 1957 *Tokugawa Religion: the values of pre-industrial Japan*. London
Bemile, S.K. 1983 *The Wisdom which Surpasses that of the King: Dàgàrà stories*. Heidelberg
Benjamin, W. [1936] 1968a The work of art in the age of mechanical reproduction. In W. Benjamin, *Illuminations: essays and reflections,* ed. H. Arendt. New York
   1968b The storyteller. In above.
Bernardi, B. 1959 *The Mugwe, A Failing Prophet: a study of a religious and public dignitary of the Meru of Kenya*. London
Boas, F. 1904 The folklore of the Eskimo. *Journal of American Folklore* 64: 1–13.
Bohannan, P. 1957 *Justice and Judgement among the Tiv*. London
Bossard, J. H. S. and Boll, E. S. 1950 *Ritual in Family Living*. Philadelphia, PA
Boyer, P. 2001 *Religion Explained: the evolutionary origins of religious thought*. New York
Braudel, F. [1971] 1981–4 *Civilization and Capitalism 15th-18th Century*. London
Caillois, R. [1939] 1959 *Man and the Sacred*. Glencoe, IL
Cardinall, A. W. 1931 *Tales Told in Togoland*. London
Cassirer, E. [1955–7] 1996 *The Philosophy of Symbolic Forms*, trans. R. Manheim. New Haven, CT
Chadwick, H. M. and N. K. 1932–40 *The Growth of Literature*, 3 vols. Cambridge

Chang, J. 1991 *Wild Swans: three daughters of China*. London

Chartier, R. 1985 Text, symbols and Frenchness: historical uses of symbolic anthropology. *Journal of Modern History* 57: 682–95

Christaller, J. G. 1879 *Twi mmebusem, mpensã-ahansĩa mmoaano: a collection of three thousand and six hundred Tshi proverbs, in use among the Negroes of the Gold Coast speaking the Asante and Fante language, collected, together with their variations, and alphabetically arranged.* Basel

Clark, K. and Holquist, M. 1984 The theory of the novel. In *Mikhail Bakhtin*. Cambridge, MA

Daniel, N. 1975 *European–Arab Relations during the Middle Ages*. London

Daniels, B. C. 1995 *Puritans at Play: leisure and recreation in Colonial New England*. New York

Darnton, R. 1984 *The Great Cat Massacre and other episodes in French cultural history*. New York

De Alfonso, P. 1977 *Disciplina Clericalis*, trans. P. R. Quarrie. London

De Brosses, C. 1760 *Du culte des dieux fétiches*. Paris

Defoe, D. 1763 *The Dreadful Visitation in a Short Account of the Progress and Effects of the Plague*. Germantown, PA

1774 *Robinson Crusoe*. New York

Derrida, J. 1978 *Writing and Difference*. London

Deshussan, P. 1998 Monologue au désert. *Le Monde*, 14 August

Deslongchamps, L. 1838 *Essai sur les fables indiennes*. Paris

Dickens, C. 1854 *Hard Times*. London

Doody, M. A. 1996 *The True Story of the Novel*. New Brunswick, NJ

Dorson, R. M. 1976 *Folklore or Fakelore?* Cambridge, MA

Dumézil, G. [1940] 1990 *Mitra-Varuna: an essay on two Indo-European representations of sovereignty*. Cambridge, MA

Dundes, A. 1980 *Interpreting Folklore*. Bloomington, IN

Durkheim, E. [1893] 1933 *The Division of Labour in Society*, trans. G. Simpson. New York

[1912] 1947 *The Elementary Forms of Religious Life*. Glencoe, IL

Edgeworth, M. 1801 *Belinda*. London

Eliade, M. 1958 *Patterns in Comparative Religion*. New York

Emmet, D. 1958 *Function, Purpose and Powers*. London

Evans-Pritchard, E. E. 1937 *Witchcraft, Oracles & Magic Among the Azande*. London

1956 *Nuer Religion*. London

1960 Introduction to Hertz, R. *Death and the Right Hand*, trans. R. Needham. London

Finnegan, R. 1970 *Oral Literature in Africa*. Oxford

Firth, R. 1959 Problem and assumption in an anthropological study of religion. *Journal of the Royal Anthropological Institute* 89: 129–48

Flaubert, G. [1857] 2003 *Madame Bovary*, trans. G. Wall. Harmondsworth
Forde, D. 1958a *The Context of Belief.* Liverpool
  1958b Spirits, witches, and sorcerors in the supernatural economy of the
  Yakō. *Journal of the Royal Anthropological Institute* 88: 165–78
Fortes, M. and Evans-Pritchard, E. E. 1940 *African Political Systems.*
  London
Frazer, J. 1890 *The Golden Bough: a study in comparative religion.* London
Fromm, E. 1957 *The Forgotten Language: an introduction to the understanding
  of dreams.* New York
Freud, S. 1975 *Psychopathology of Everyday Life.* Harmondsworth
Furet, F. and Ozouf, J. 1977 *Lire et écrire: l'alphabétisation des français de
  Calvin à Jules Ferry.* Paris
Gandah, S. W. D. K. 2004 *The Silent Rebel.* Legon: Institute of African
  Studies
Giddens, A. 1991 *Modernity and Self-identity.* Stanford, CA
Ginsberg, C. 1980 *The Cheese and the Worms.* London
Gluckman, M. 1965 *Custom and Conflict in Africa.* Oxford
Goode, W. J. 1951 *Religion among the Primitives.* Glencoe, IL
Goody, J. R. 1957 Anomie in Ashanti? *Africa* 27: 75–104
  1961 Religion and ritual: the definitional problem. *British Journal of
  Sociology* 12: 142–63
  1972 *The Myth of the Bagre.* Oxford
  1977a Tradizione orale e ricostruzione del passata nel Ghana del Nord.
  Quaderni Storici 35: 481–92
  1977b *The Domestication of the Savage Mind.* Cambridge
  1986 *The Logic of Writing and the Organisation of Society.* Cambridge
  1987 *The Interface between the Written and the Oral.* Cambridge
  1990 *The Oriental, the Ancient, and the Primitive.* Cambridge
  1997a *Representations and Contradictions: ambivalence towards images,
  theatre, fiction, relics and sexuality.* Oxford
  1997b *The Culture of Flowers.* Cambridge
  1998 *Food and Love.* London
  2009a *Renaissances: the one or the many?* Cambridge
  2009b *The Eurasian Miracle.* Cambridge
Goody, J. R. and Gandah, S. W. D. K. (eds.) 1981 *Une Récitation du Bagré.*
  Paris
  (eds.) 2002 *A Myth Revisited: The Third Bagre.* Durham, NC
Goody, J. R. and Goody, E. 1991 Creating a text: alternative interpretations
  of Gonja drum history. *Africa* 62: 266–70
Goody, J. R. and Watt, I. 1963 The consequences of literacy. *Comparative
  Studies in Society and History* 5: 304–45
Gough, K. 1981 *Rural Society in Southeast India.* Cambridge
Graves, R. [1955] 1992 *The Greek Myths.* Harmondsworth

Grimm, J. and W. 1819 *Kinder- und Hausmärchen*, 3 vols. Berlin

Hägg, T. 1983 *The Novel in Antiquity*. Oxford

Hall, S. 1984 The narrative structure of reality. *Southern Review*, Adelaide, 17: 3–17

Harrison, J. E. 1912 *Themis*. Cambridge

Hartman, G. H. 1999 The struggle for the text. In *A Critic's Journey, 1958–1998*. New Haven, CT

Hegel, R. E. 1981 *The Novel in Seventeenth-century China*. New York

Heiserman, A. 1977 *The Novel before the Novel*. Chicago

Hertz, R. [1907] 1960 *Death and the Right Hand*, trans. R. Needham. London

Hiskett, M. 1957 Material relating to state of learning among the Fulani before the Jihad. *Bulletin SOAS* 19: 550–78

Hobsbawm, E. 1959 *Primitive Rebels: studies in archaic forms of social movement in the 19th and 20th centuries*. Manchester

Hodgkin, T. 1966 The Islamic literary tradition in Ghana. In I. M. Lewis (ed.), *Islam in Tropical Africa*. London

Holzberg, N. 1995 *The Ancient Novel: an introduction*. Chicago

Hooke, S. H. 1958 *Myth, Ritual and Kingship*. Oxford

Horton, R. 1960 A definition of religion, and its uses. *Journal of the Royal Anthropological Institute* 90: 201–26

Jacobs, A. 2007 *On Matricide: myth, psychoanalysis, and the law of the mother*. New York

Jameson, F. 1981 *The Political Unconscious: narrative as a socially symbolic act*. London

Jardine, L. and Brotton, J. 2000 *Global Interests: Renaissance art between east and west*. London

Keats, J. 1982 *Complete Poems*, ed. J. Stillinger. Cambridge, MA

Kettle, A. 1965 Emma. In I. Watt (ed.), *Jane Austen: a collection of critical essays*. Englewood Cliffs, NJ

Kluckhorn, C. 1952 Values and value-orientations in the theory of action: an exploration in definition and classification. In T. Parsons and E. A. Shils (eds.), *Towards a General Theory of Action*. Cambridge, MA

Kuhn, T. S. 1962 *The Structure of Scientific Revolutions*. Chicago

Lang, A. 1893. Introduction to M. R. Cox, *Cinderella, 345 Variants* (Folklore Society Monograph series, no. 31). London

Leach, E. R. 1954 *Political Systems of Highland Burma*. London

Leavis, Q. D. 1932 *Fiction and the Reading Public*. London

Leites, N. and Bernaut, E. 1954 *Ritual of Liquidation: communists on trial*. Glencoe, IL

Lennox, C. 1752 *The Female Quixote*. London

Leroy, J. 1985 *Fabricated World: an interpretation of Kewa tales*. Vancouver

Le Roy Ladurie, E. [1975] 1978 *Montaillou: Cathars and Catholics in a French village, 1294–1324*, trans. B. Bray. London

Lessa, W. A. and Vogt, E. Z. 1958 *Reader in Comparative Religion*. Evanston, IL

Lévi-Strauss, C. 1956 Les organisations dualistes existent-elles? *Bijdragen tot de Taal-, Land- en Volkenkunde* 112: 99–128

1961 La Geste d'Asdiwal. *Les Temps Modernes* 16: 1080–1123

1964 *Totemism*, trans. R. Needham. London

1966 *The Savage Mind*, trans. J. and D. Weightman. London

1968 The structural study of myth. In *Structural Anthropology*. London

1969 *Mythologiques*. Paris

Lévy-Bruhl, L. 1923 *Primitive Mentality*, trans. L. A. Clare. London

Lewis, G. 2000 *A Failure of Treatment*. Oxford

Lewis, I. M. (ed.) 1966 *Islam in Tropical Africa*. London

Lloyd, G. E. R. 1990 *Demystifying Mentalities*. Cambridge

1991 *Methods and Problems in Greek Science*. Cambridge

Lönnrot, E. [1849] 1989 *The Kalevala: an epic poem after oral tradition*, trans. K. Bosley. Oxford

Lord, A. B. 1960 *The Singer of Tales*. Cambridge, MA

Lowie, R. H. 1935 *The Crow Indians*. New York

Macfarlane, A. 1978 *The Origins of English Individualism; the family, property and social transition*. Oxford

Maine, H. S. 1861 *Ancient Law*. London

Malinowski, B. 1922 *Argonauts of the Western Pacific: an account of native enterprise and adventure in the archipelagoes of Melanesian New Guinea*. London

1926 *Myth in Primitive Psychology*. London

1954 *Magic, Science and Religion: and other essays*. New York

Marett, R. R. 1914 *The Threshold of Religion*. London

Mather, I. 1693 *A Further Account of the Tryals of the New-England Witches … To which is added, Cases of conscience concerning witchcrafts and evil spirits personating men*. London

McKillop, A. D. 1963 Critical realism in *Northanger Abbey*. In I. Watt (ed.), *Jane Austen: a collection of critical essays*. Englewood Cliffs, NJ

McMullen, J. 1999 *Idealism, Protest and the Tale of Genji: the Confucianism of Kumazawa Banzan*. Oxford

Merlan, F. 1995 Indigenous narrative genres in the Highlands of Papua New Guinea. In P. Silberman and J. Loftlin (eds.), *Proceedings of the Second Annual Symposium about Language and Society*. Austin, TX

Mintz, S. W. 1985 *Sweetness and Power: the place of sugar in modern history*. New York

Morgan, J. R. and Stoneman, R. (eds.) 1994 *Greek Fiction: the Greek novel in context*. London

Morris, C. 1946 *Signs, Language and Behaviour.* New York
Nadel, S. F. 1954 *Nupe Religion.* London
Needham, R. 1960 The Left Hand of the Mugwe: an analytical note on the structure of Meru symbolism. *Africa* 30: 28–33
Nicole, P. 1667 *Les Visionnaires.* Liège
Orwell, G. 1968 Looking back on the Spanish War. In S. Orwell and I. Angus (eds.), *Collected Essays.* London
Page, D. 1973 *Folktales in Homer's Odyssey.* Cambridge, MA
Parry, M. 1971 *The Making of Homeric Verse*, ed. A. Parry. Oxford
Parsons, T. 1954 *The Structure of Social Action.* New York
Parsons, T. and Shils, E. 1952 Values, motives and systems of action. In T. Parsons and E. A. Shils (eds.), *Towards a General Theory of Society.* Cambridge, MA
Paulme, D. 1967 Two themes on the origin of death in West Africa. *Man* n.s. 2: 48–61
Perrault, C. 1959 *Contes en vers. Contes de ma mère. l'Oie… ou l'Histoires ou contes du temps passé.* Strasbourg
Perry, B. E. 1967 *The Ancient Romances: a literary-historical account of their origins.* Berkeley, CA
Perry, R. B. 1926 *General theory of value: its meaning and basic principles construed in terms of interest.* New York
Plaks, A. H. (ed.) 1977 *Chinese Narrative: critical and theoretical essays.* Princeton, NJ
Propp, V. 1968 *Morphology of the Folktale* (2nd edn). Austin, TX
Radcliffe-Brown, A. R. 1950 Introduction *African Systems of Kinship and Marriage*, ed. D. Forde and A. R. Radcliffe-Brown. London
    1952 *Structure and Function in Primitive Society.* London
    1993 *The Andaman Islanders* (2nd edn). London
Radin, P. 1956 *The Trickster: a study in American Indian mythology.* London
Rattray, R. S. 1932 *The Tribes of the Ashanti Hinterland.* Oxford
Richardson, S. 1741 *Pamela: or, virtue rewarded.* London
    1748 *Clarissa.* London
Robertson-Smith, W. 1889 *Lectures on the Religion of the Semites.* London
Rumsey, A. 2006 Verbal art, politics, and personal style in Highland New Guinea and beyond. In C. O'Neil, K. J. Tuite and M. Scoggin (eds.), *Language, Culture and the Individual: a tribute to Paul Friedrich.* Munich
Schapera, I. 1956 *Government and Politics in Tribal Societies.* London
Scott, J. C. 1976 *The Moral Economy of the Peasant.* New Haven, CT
    1985 *Weapons of the Weak: everyday forms of peasant resistance.* London
Scribner, S. and Cole, M. 1981 *The Psychology of Literacy.* London.
Seydou, C. (ed.) 1972 *Silâmaka et Poullôri.* Paris
Siran, J-L. 1998 *L'Illusion mythique.* Paris

Somé, M. 1994 *Of Water and the Spirit: magic and initiation in the life of an African shaman.* New York

Sommerville, C. J. 1996 *The News Revolution in England: cultural dynamics of daily information.* Oxford

Staffe, La Baronne 1892 *Lady's Dressing Room,* trans. Lady C. Campbell. London

Tatum, J. A. (ed.) 1994 *The Search for the Ancient Novel.* Baltimore

Tedlock, D. 1983 *The Spoken Word and the Work of Interpretation.* Philadelphia, PA

Thompson, E. P. 1963 *The Making of the English Working Class.* London

Thompson, S. 1951 *The Folktale.* New York

1955–8. *Motif-index of Folk-literature: a classification of narrative elements in folktales, ballads, myths, fables, medieval romances, exempla, fabliaux, jest-books, and local legends.* 6 vols. Revised and enlarged. Copenhagen

Thoms, W. 1846 Letter (August 22) to the *Athenaeum.* London

Tillich, P. 1951–63 *Systematic Theology,* 3 vols. Chicago

Tylor, E. B. 1871 *Primitive Culture: researches into the development of mythology, philosophy, religion, language, art and custom.* London

Veillard, G. 1931 Récits peuls du Macina et du Kunari. *Bulletin du comité d'études historiques et scientifiques de l'Afrique Occidentales Française* 14: 137–56

Wallerstein, I. 1999 The West, capitalism, and the modern world-system. In T. Brook and G. Blue (eds.), *China and Historical Capitalism.* Cambridge

Walpole, H. 1903 *The Letters of Horace Walpole, Fourth Earl of Orford,* vol. 11: *1743–1750,* ed. P. Toynbee. Oxford

Ward, B. 1956 Some observations on religious cults in Ashanti. *Africa* 26: 47–61.

Warner, W. L. 1937 *A Black Civilization.* New York

Weber, M. 1946 *Essays in Sociology,* trans. H. Gerth and C. W. Mills. New York

1947 *The Theory of Social and Economic Organisation,* trans. A. M. Henderson and T. Parsons. Edinburgh

Wilks, I. 1963 The growth of Islamic learning in Ghana. *Journal of the Historical Society of Nigeria* 2: 409–17

Wilson, M. 1957 *Rituals of Kinship among the Nyakusa.* London

Winch, P. 1958 *The Idea of a Social Science and Its Relation to Philosophy.* London

Wolf, E. R. 1982 *Europe and the Peoples Without History.* Berkeley, CA

Worsley, P. 1957 *The Trumpet Shall Sound: a study of 'cargo cults' in Melanesia.* New York

Žanic, I. 1998 *Prevarena povijest.* Zagreb

Index

acts of propitiation
  and religious activity, 33–4
Aesop's fables, 49
Alfonso, Pedro de, 136
allegory, 49
Analects, 144
analytic concepts
  definition, 14
analytical problems
  creation of mythology from various
    sources, 99
Ananse stories, 4, 48, 86, 131
Andaman Islanders, 2
animals
  characteristics of LoDagaa and Gonja
    myths, 85–6
  characters in LoDagaa and Gonja myths,
    86, 87
  in folktales, 55–6
animatism, 15
animism, 1, 15
Annales school, 81
anthropology
  impact of audio recording, 58–63
approaches to the study of myth
  and ritual, 1–2
Arabian Nights, 136, 146
Arreto, 137
Asante, 48, 65, 86
audience
  for oral genres, 79–81
  influence on the performance, 61
audio recording
  impact on analysis of oral literature, 63
  impact on anthropology, 58–63
  limitations of earlier written
    recording, 61
Austen, Jane, 140–2

Australian Aborigines, 52, 53
Azande, 1, 30
  witchcraft, 23, 24–5

Bagre of the LoDagaa, 2–3, 7–8, 10–11, 46,
    81, 128, 153
  Black Bagre, 65–6, 98–9, 110–11, 129–30
  content of recitations, 116
  context, 61, 107–9
  cultural transmission, 104–7
  differences between versions, 63, 65–6
  discovery of change through creativity, 63
  distinction between myth and
    mythology, 100
  early recording methods, 61
  impact of audio recording on analysis, 63
  importance to social science, 97–8
  influence of the audience, 61
  lack of a category term for
    their myth, 101
  limitations of written records, 61
  Myth of the Bagre, 128–30, 155
  narratives within, 128–30
  notion of recitation, 100
  objections to the term 'myth', 101–2
  oral creativity, 63, 65–6
  personnel, 109–10
  purpose and functions, 128–30
  thought (mentality) of oral
    cultures, 102
  variations over time and space, 102–4
  versions recorded in the field, 95–7
  White Bagre, 66, 98, 110–11, 129–30
Bakhtin, Mikhail, 118
Baktaman of New Guinea, 105
ballad, 50
Behn, Aphra, 138
beings of the wild (fairies), 88

174

Belinda, 142
Bemba, 49
Benjamin, Walter, 117, 133, 147
Beowulf, 44, 45
Bergson, Henri-Louis, 17
Bete of the Ivory Coast, 90, 91
Bible, 43, 45, 49, 76, 128, 129, 133, 153, 157
Black Bagre, 65–6, 98–9, 110–11, 129–30
Boccaccio, Giovanni, 137
Book of Sinbad, The, 136
Bovarism, 135, 142
'boxed' stories, 136–7
Boyer, Pascal, 104–7
Brahmans, 43, 65, 160
Brer Rabbit, 131
Breton lays, 44
Bronte family, 146
Buddhism, 15–16, 81
Bunyan, John, 138

Canterbury Tales, 137
Cassirer, Ernst, 2
category term (genre name) for myths, 101
ceremonial
    and religious activity, 17–20
    and ritual, 36
    definition, 36
    variations and modifications, 66–7
Cervantes, Miguel de, 140
chant, 50
Chaucer, Geoffrey, 137
children
    conceptual simplification in stories, 89–91
    folktales and stories for, 47–9, 130–1
    rhymes and songs for, 48
    versions of stories for, 8–9, 11
Christianity
    story of, 4
Clarissa, 138
cognitive approach to myth and ritual, 1–2
collective unconscious
    myth as window on, 6–7, 10
Coming of the Kusiele (clan legend), 99
Confessio Amantis, 137
contemporary myth, 7–8
content of oral literature, 55–7
contes de fées (fairy tales), 47–8, 73–4, 156
context
    of oral genres, 79–81
    of recitations, 61
Corde Lucaver, el, 137
creativity, *see* oral creativity

cross-continental transformation of myths, 4
Crow Indians, 74, 80
cult of the dead
    and religion, 15
cultural history
    and folktales, 70–83
Cultural Revolution, 146
cultural transmission, 104–7

Dakota, 15, 16
Daphne and Chloe, 136
Darnton, Robert, 70–83
Dawkins, Richard, 104
Decameron, 137
defining analytic concepts
    challenges in social science, 14
Defoe, Daniel, 138, 139
Dickens, Charles, 146
Discipline Clericalis, 136
Dogon myth, 100, 101
Don Quixote, 140
*Dreadful Visitation in a Short Account
    of the Progress and Effects of the Plague,
    The* 139
drum histories, 54, 103
Dumézil, Georges, 5
Durkheim, Émile, 15–16, 17–33, 37–40

Edgeworth, Maria, 142
Eliot, George, 146
emotive criteria for religion, 16
epic, 43–4
    content of, 55
    narratives in oral cultures, 121–7
    oral and written forms, 44–6
Eskimo, 64, 69
euhemerism, 1
Evans-Pritchard, E. E., 1, 16, 23, 24–5, 30, 34

fables
    oral genre, 49
fairies (beings of the wild), 88
fairy tales (*contes de fées*), 47–8, 73–4, 156
Fang, 123
fantasy in narrative, 120
Female Quixote, The, 140
fictional narrative, 120–1
Fielding, Henry, 138
Finnegan, Ruth, 122–4
Flaubert, Gustave, 142–3
folk drama, 51–2
folklore, 43

folktales
  and cultural history, 70–83
  and myth, 52
  animals in, 55–6
  audience for, 79–81
  choice of characters, 92–4
  comparing LoDagaa and Gonja, 84–94
  content of, 55
  context, 79–81
  continuity of form and content, 12
  distinction from myths, 8–9, 11
  for children, 47–9, 130–1
  in northern Ghana, 11
  internationalization, 11
  oral genre, 47–9
  performance, 55
  psychoanalytic interpretation, 78–9
  range and vagueness of definitions, 79–81
  similar tales in dissimilar social systems,
    91–2
Food and Love, 107
forgetting
  and creativity in recitations, 66
Frazer, James, 2, 22, 23–4, 34, 36, 76
Freud, Sigmund, 8, 10, 131
Fromm, Erich, 78–9
Fulani epic of Silâmaka and Poullôri, 125–6
functionalist approach to myth and ritual,
    1–2, 59
funeral ceremonies, 66–7

Gandah, Kum, 65, 95, 96
ghosts, 85, 88
Gilgamesh epic, 45, 50, 123, 128, 131
gods
  characteristics in LoDagaa and Gonja
    myths, 85–6
  in LoDagaa and Gonja myth, 87–8
Golden Ass, The, 118, 136
Gonja drum histories, 54, 103
Gonja folktales, 11
  animal characters, 85–6, 87
  categories of characters, 85–6
  comparison with LoDagaa
    folktales, 84–94
  conceptual simplification, 90–1
  gods as characters, 85–6, 87–8
  interaction between categories of
    characters, 88
  men as characters, 85–7
Gonja society, 84
Gothic novels, 140–2

Graves, Robert, 4
Great Divide between the enlightened and
    unenlightened, 73, 76, 102
Greek mythology, 4, 5–8, 9
Grimm brothers, 79, 81, 131
griots of Bambara and Mali, 123, 124–6
guslari (Balkans), 76, 77

Harrison, Jane, 13–14
hierarchical dualism in myth, 5, 7
historical recitations (histories)
  oral genre, 53–5
history
  distinction from myth, 120
Holdesheimer, Wolfgang, 149
Holocaust, 149
Homer, 43, 44, 45, 46, 76, 81, 117, 120, 122,
    150, 160

Iliad, 42
Indian epics, 150
Indo-European myth, 5
Islam, 81, 84, 87, 122, 124, 125, 146, 154
  story of, 4

Jacobs, A., 4–7
Jin Ping Mei (*The Golden Lotus*), 144, 148
Joyce, James, 148
Judaism, 146

Kalevala, 45
Kalila wa Dimna, 136
Kandinsky, Wassily, 148
Keats, John, 150–1
Kipling, Rudyard, 47

lecto-oral societies, 51, 73, 123
lecto-oral transmission, 41–2, 155–6, 161
legends
  definition of, 11
  narratives in oral cultures, 127–8
  oral genre, 53–5
Lennox, Charlotte, 140
Lévi-Strauss, Claude, 2, 3–4, 5, 6, 10, 37, 52,
    59, 93, 98, 133
Lévy-Bruhl, Lucien, 23, 103
Lewis, Gilbert, 11, 132
Lianja epic, 123
literacy
  impact on oral cultures, 8
literature
  use of the term for oral genres, 41–2

'Little Red Riding Hood', 73, 78
LoDagaa folktales
  animal characters, 85–6, 87
  categories of characters, 85–6
  comparison with Gonja
    folktales, 84–94
  conceptual simplification, 90–1
  gods as characters, 85–6, 87–8
  interaction between categories of
    characters, 88
  men as characters, 85–7
LoDagaa narratives
  distinction between truth and falsehood,
    120–1
LoDagaa, 25, 30
  arrangement of society, 84
  concept of medicine, 17
  folktales, 11
  mythology, 3
  study of their myth or recitation, 1
  see also Bagre of the LoDagaa
Lord's Prayer, 154, 157
Love and Friendship, 142

Madame Bovary, 142–3
magic
  distinction from religion, 13–33
magico-religious behaviour
  and ritual, 34–5
  attempts to define, 13–33
Mahabharata, 128
Malevich, Kazimir, 148
Malinowski, Bronisław, 2, 16, 21, 22, 23–4,
  25, 52, 59, 93
Maori haka, 50
Marett, R. R., 15, 16, 17, 34
matricide, 4–7
means–end schema, 29–30
Melanesian people, 15, 16
memes, 104–6
memorizing written texts, 159–60
men
  in LoDagaa and Gonja myths, 85–7
Meredith, George, 146
Merry Adventures of Emperor Yang, The, 145
Meru people, 38
Ming literati novels, 137
Mongo-Nkundo tales, 123
Mungo epic, 131
Murngin, 18, 39
music
  invention and change, 99–100

myth
  as a body of mythology (myth 2), 3–4, 6
  as a specific recital (myth 1), 2–3, 7–8
  as a specific recitation in all its versions
    (myth 3), 4–7
  as an oral genre, 52–3
  as cultural delirium, 6–7
  challenges of study, 6, 9
  changes over time, 9–11
  child and adult interpretations, 8–9
  content of, 55
  creativity and variation, 2–3
  cross-continental transformation, 4
  distinction from folktales, 8–9, 11
  distinction from history, 120
  distinction from mythology, 100, 128
  distribution of myths, 128
  functions of myths, 128–30
  interpretation of the believer's view, 6–7
  narrative content, 128–30
  objections to use of the term, 101–2
  performance, 55
  plurality of versions, 6, 7–8, 9
  search for a collective unconscious,
    6–7, 10
  transcendental view, 4
  unconscious element, 5–7, 10
  variability of form and content, 12
  variants of a particular story, 2–3
  variations between continents, 4
myth and ritual school, 98
Myth of the Bagre, 128–30, 155
mytheopoeic thinking, 2
mythology
  construction by observers, 100
  creation of, 99
  distinction from myth, 100, 128

Nadel, S. F., 30, 31, 35
Nambikwara mythology, 3–4
Nancy tales, 48, 131
narrative
  all-inclusive definitions, 118–19
  distinction between truth and falsehood,
    119–21
  effects of introduction of writing, 133–5
  fantasy, 120
  fictional, 120–1
  influence of writing, 154
  narrower definition, 118
  personal, 131–2
  see also novels; storytelling

narratives in oral cultures, 8
  epics, 121–7
  lack of prominence, 132–3
  legends, 127–8
  recited myths, 128–30
Navajo people, 49, 52
non-rational (transcendental)
  action, 29–30
Northanger Abbey, 140–1
Novella, 137
novels
  'boxed' stories, 136–7
  criticisms of, 146
  development of the narrative, 154
  early narratives, 135–6
  effects of the introduction of writing,
    133–5
  fancy and fantasy, 150–1
  Gothic novels, 140–2
  history of, 152
  influence of development of printing,
    133–4
  leading women astray, 143
  objections to, 146
  origins of the term, 135
  problem of acceptability, 135
  romantic novels, 143
  timing of appearance, 118
  works of Jane Austen, 140–2
Nuer, 16, 30
Nupe, 30, 31, 35
nursery rhymes, 48
nursery tales, 73–4

Odyssey, 45
Oedipus story, 4, 6–8
Of Water and the Spirit, 121
ontological categories, 106–7
oral creativity, 64
  Bagre of the LoDagaa, 65–6
  ceremonies, 66–7
  effects of forgetting, 66
  recitations, 65–6
  variations in myths, 2–3
oral cultures
  distinction between truth and falsehood,
    120–1
  impact of literacy, 8
  lack of prominence of narrative, 132–3
  mentality (thought), 102
  role of narrative, 8
oral genres, 42, 46–7

allegory, 49
  audience for, 79–81
  children's folktales and stories, 47–9
  context, 79–81
  epic, 44–6
  fables, 49
  folk drama, 51–2
  folktales, 47–9
  historical recitations (histories), 53–5
  legends, 53–5
  myth, 52–3
  range and vagueness of definitions, 79–81
  songs and singing, 50–1
  theatre, 51–2
oral literature, 41–57
  content, 55–7
  context of performance, 57
  distinction from written literature, 46
  distribution of different genres, 56
  folklore, 43
  impact of writing, 42–6
  meaning of the term, 42
  performance, 44, 55
  supernatural characters, 57
  truth status of different genres, 56–7
  use of the term 'literature', 41–2
  see also oral genres
oral memorization
  effects of writing, 159–61
oral recitations
  comparison with religious texts, 154–5
oral societies
  agricultural technology, 69
  diversity of religious activities, 69
  static view of, 64
  variations in ritual and religion, 64–5
Oresteian story, 5–6
Orwell, George, 119
Othello, 148

parables, 49
Parry, Milman, 44
Parsons, Talcott, 15, 17, 21, 22, 23–4, 26, 27,
  28–30
performance of oral literature, 55
Perrault, Charles, 47–8, 75–6, 156
personal narratives, 131–2
Pilgrim's Progress, 138
Plato, 150, 151, 152
Political Unconscious, The, 118
Prayer Mat of Flesh, The, 145
prayers, 154

'primitive mind' concept, 2
'primitive society'
    association with myth and ritual, 1–2
printing
    and the appearance of the novel, 133–4
    effect on storytelling, 133
    influence of, 138
Propp, Vladimir, 78
psychoanalysis, 131
    interpretation of folktales, 78–9
Puritanical Complex, 139

Quran, 45, 76, 125, 156, 157

Radcliffe-Brown, A. R., 2, 17, 20, 21,
    26–8, 36
reading aloud, 161
recitation
    meanings of the term, 100
    of oral literature, 100
    see also Bagre of the LoDagaa
religious activity
    acts of propitiation, 33–4
    and ceremonials, 17–20
    and the cult of the dead, 15
    and ultimate values of society, 28–9
    attempts to define, 13–33
    definition, 33–4
    distinction from magic, 13–33
    diversity of approaches, 69
    emotive criteria, 16
    exclusive definition, 15–16
    inclusive definition, 15–16, 17–33
    Marett's definition, 15
    negative criteria for, 29–30
    non-rational (transcendental) action,
        29–30
    practices outside the intrinsic means–end
        schema, 29–30
    sacred–profane dichotomy, 15–16, 37–40
    Tylor's definition, 15–16
religious texts
    comparison with oral recitations, 154–5
Representations and Contradictions, 106, 107
research
    conceptual simplifications given to the
        researcher, 90–1
    decontextualization of recitations, 61
    impact of tape recording on analysis, 63
    limitations of written records, 61
rhetoric, 44
Richardson, Samuel, 138

Rig Veda, 65, 81, 160
ritual
    and ceremonial, 36
    and magico-religious behaviour, 34–5
    and myth, 52
    as performance, 51
    attempts to define, 13–33
    definition, 34–5, 36–7
    types of, 36–7
Robertson Smith, W., 16, 17, 19
Robinson Crusoe, 138, 139
Roman Catholic Church, 54, 56
romantic novels, 143
Romulus and Remus, 55
Rowling, J. K., 42, 49
Russian folktales, 78

sacred–profane dichotomy, 15–16, 21–33,
    37–40
saints' stories, 54, 56
schools
    and the emergence of writing, 153
    development of, 153
Scott, Walter, 146, 147
Sércambi, Giovanni, 137
Seven Sages, The, 136
shrines, 66–9
Siran, J. L., 100–2
Smollett, Tobias, 138
Somé, Malidoma, 121
songs and singing, 50–1
    children's rhymes and songs, 48
    invention and change, 99–100
speech
    relation to writing, 42–4
spider stories, 86, 131
spiritual agencies, 17
spiritual beings
    belief in, 15
standardized oral forms, 42
storytelling
    impact of printing, 117
    in oral cultures, 117
    see also narrative
structuralist approach to myth and ritual,
    1–2, 3, 4–6, 59
supernatural agencies, 17

Tale of Bergis, 137
Tale of Genji, The, 144, 145
theatre, 51–2
Thompson, Stith, 79–81

thought (mentality) of oral cultures, 102
Thousand and One Nights, The, 146
Tokugawa religion, 29
totemism, 4, 55
traditional societies
     assumptions about the nature of, 102–4
     comparison with modern
          societies, 102–4
transcendental action, 29–30
transcendental view of mythology, 4
trickster characters, 56, 86, 131
Trobriand Islanders, 2, 22, 23–4, 25
Trollope, Anthony, 146
truth and untruth in narrative, 119–21
Tylor, E. B., 15–16, 22, 34

ultimate values of society
     and religion, 28–9
unconscious element in myth, 5–7, 10

Vai of West Africa, 153
values of society
     and religion, 28–9
Vedas, 43, 45, 46, 160
veillées, 75–6

Water Margin, 145
Watt, Ian, 13
Weber, Max, 22, 31, 32, 102
White Bagre, 66, 98, 110–11, 129–30
Wilson, Monica, 36

Woolf, Virginia, 148
writing
     and development of schools, 153
     and development of the narrative, 154
     and oral memory, 159–61
     development of scripts, 154
     emergence of, 154
     influence on the narrative, 133–5
     influence on the novel, 133–5
     lecto-oral transmission, 155–6, 161
     memorizing written texts, 159–60
     rapid reading, 160–1
     relation to speech, 42–4
     religious texts, 154–5
     scanning a text for meaning, 160–1
     social implications, 153
     standardization in the written
          system, 161
     see also novels
written literature
     distinction from oral literature, 46
written records of recitations
     limitations of, 61

xylophone music
     invention and change, 99–100

Yakö, 39

Zuni of North America, 128